John Freeman

Brotherhood Program of a Baptist Church

Compiled By
NORMAN GODFREY and
ROY JENNINGS

PRINCIPLES FOR EDUCATING AND INVOLVING BAPTIST MEN AND BOYS IN MISSIONS

Revised 1969

Code Number: **Church Study Course**
This book is number 6601 of the Christian Leadership Series

Library of Congress catalog card number: 76–101633
Printed in the United States of America

Revised and Reprinted, March, 1970
Reprinted, November, 1970

Foreword

• Centuries ago Christ commanded his followers to "go into all the world" and share their faith "with all peoples." That charge positionized clearly and for all time the work of every Christian. Christ implied each Christian is to share his faith as effectively as possible at every opportunity without exception.

In the Great Commission, Christ also was saying Christians carry deep and significant obligations which demand involvement—of the whole of life.

The true value of the life of a Christian is reflected in his witness and ministry to persons in the name of his Lord.

But the command of Christ extends beyond those areas a Christian can reach personally. The message of Christ is for all peoples. It knows no boundaries. That includes all persons regardless of nationality, race, culture, or status in life. To obey Christ at this point a Christian is obligated to lock hands, hearts, prayers, and assets with other Christians in a joint effort. This is how a Christian fulfills Christ's mission in the world.

Brotherhood work among Southern Baptists seeks to help churches perform their tasks of teaching missions to men and boys, engaging them in mission action, and leading them to support world missions through prayer and giving.

The units of work within Brotherhood—Baptist Men and Royal Ambassadors—are simply means through which the church does this job. A Brotherhood in a Baptist church is never an end within itself. It justifies its existence only when it performs at its maximum in achieving the purposes the church has assigned to it.

The purpose of this book is to define and describe the work of the Brotherhood in a Baptist church. It covers (1) the basic reasons why a church needs a Brotherhood, (2) how the church can organize or group men and boys to do its work, (3) duties of the leaders of the units of Brotherhood work, and (4) ways men and boys can witness and minister to people of special need and circumstance in the name of Christ.

The message of the book is more than the mechanics of operating a Brotherhood program in a Baptist church. It seeks to make clear the role of the laity in the work of churches. These understandings by men and boys are sorely needed if they are to be challenged and involved in church-centered actions designed to witness and minister to people of special need and circumstance in today's world.

I commend this book to every Southern Baptist pastor and Brotherhood leader. Properly applied, the suggested organizational patterns, coupled with well prepared leadership and adequate planning, can make Brotherhood a series of meaningful and effective experiences in missions for men and boys in any church. It is the desire and prayer of all who contributed to the book that it will achieve this end.

George W. Schroeder
Executive Secretary
Brotherhood Commission,
Southern Baptist Convention

Acknowledgements

• Contents of this book were compiled by Norman Godfrey and Roy Jennings of the Brotherhood Commission staff.

The compilers got much of their basic information from the 1966 edition of *The Brotherhood Program of a Baptist Church,* by George L. Euting, vice-president of Bluefield (Va.) College and former program development director of the Brotherhood Commission.

The material was refined and updated as needed and new information added to provide men and boys guidance in missions in the 1970s.

Mr. Godfrey is assistant to the executive secretary of the Brotherhood Commission. Mr. Jennings is program manager.

Contents

Requirements for Credit

• This book is the text for course number 7601, Subject Area 7 of the Christian Leadership Series, New Church Study Course.

Persons can earn credit for this book the following ways in these amounts:

Event	*Credits*
Class study for 2½ hours	1
Class study for 5 hours	2
Individual study (completing questions, exercises	2
Reading only	1
SBC, state assemblies, seminars, workshops.	1 (each 2½ hours of class time)

If credit is desired for this course through class study, individual study, or by reading, the following requirements must be met:

I. CLASSWORK

1. The class must meet the number of hours for the amount of credit desired. The required time does not include assembly periods. For courses in which laboratory experience or practice is desirable, two hours of such guided experience may be substituted as one hour of class time, provided at least half of the required clock hours are actually spent in classwork. The teacher will indicate the length of the class and the number of credits to be granted on the Request for Credit form.

2. A class member who attends all class sessions and completes the reading of the book as directed by the teacher will not be required to do any written work for credit.

3. A class member who is absent from one or more sessions must complete the required exercises or questions in the "Personal Learning Activities" section on all chapters he misses. In such a case, he must turn in his paper by the date the teacher sets (usually within a week or ten days following the last class). Also, he must certify that he has read the book.

4. The teacher should request an award for himself. A person who teaches a course for Youth or Adults (in any subject area) will be granted the same number of credits as class members.

5. The Training Union director or the teacher should complete the "Request for Course Credit" (Form 151) and forward it after completion of the class to the Church Study Course Awards Office, 127 Ninth Avenue, North, Nashville, Tennessee 37203.

II. INDIVIDUAL STUDY

1. A person who wishes to complete this course without attending class sessions may receive full credit by certifying he has read the book and by completing all exercises or questions in the "Personal Learning Activities" section.

2. Students may find profit in studying the text together, but individual papers are required. Carbon copies or duplicates of the answers cannot be accepted.

3. The work required for individual study credit should be turned in for checking to the Training Union director

or the person designated by the church to administer the Christian Leadership Series. The form entitled "Request for Course Credit" (Form 151) must be used in requesting these awards. It is to be forwarded by the Training Union director or the person designated by the Church Study Course Awards Office, 127 Ninth Avenue, North, Nashville, Tennessee 37203.

III. READING CREDIT

1. A person may receive one credit toward the certificates (or diploma) on which he is working by reading this book.
2. Upon completion of the reading, he must complete Request for Course Credit (Form 151). He should give the completed form to the Training Union director or to the person designated by his church to be responsible for administering the Christian Leadership Series.
3. The Training Union director or the person designated by the church will see that the request is completed, signed, and forwarded to the Church Study Course Awards Office, 127 Ninth Avenue, North, Nashville, Tennessee 37203.

IV. AWARDS AND RECORDS

Two copies of the course credit award, will be sent by the Church Study Course Awards Office to the church. One copy should be filed in the church training record and the other given to the individual.

1. The Church, Its Functions and Tasks

CHAPTER OUTLINE

A. THE CHURCH

1. What Is a Church?
2. The Nature of a Church
3. Mission of a Church

B. THE FUNCTIONS OF A CHURCH

1. Explanation of the Functions
2. Implementation of the Functions
3. Brotherhood Program

• The role of the church often becomes the subject of debate by Christians and non-Christians alike when issues arise. Take the conversation which follows:

"'What do you think should be the task of the church during this crisis?' queried a layman of his pastor in the dark days of World War II. 'The same that it was before the war started and the same that it will be once the war is over—to lead men to life in Christ,' was the forthright answer."[1]

The task of a church has not changed. There are times when men neglect or obscure this truth by giving their main attention to other things.

However, an understanding of the church and the work Jesus gave it to do is necessary for men to serve Christ effectively. The source book for understanding the church and its tasks in the world is the Bible.

A. THE CHURCH

1. What Is a Church?

The word "church" is used to translate the Greek word *ecclesia* which basically means a gathering of citizens summoned or called out by a herald to meet in a public place for some special purpose. The New Testament identifies this word with Christian believers in a stated place as, "Unto the church of God which is at Corinth" (1 Corinthians 1:2). The word is applied to a portion of the Christians in any city who assemble in a private house, ". . . with the church that is in the house" (1 Corinthians 16:19; Romans 16:5; Colossians 4:15).

The earliest churches probably met in private homes in keeping with the custom of the times. There is evidence that

[1] H. Leo Eddleman, *Missionary Task of a Church,* p. 47.

a church met in the house of Mary, mother of John Mark (Acts 12:12); and in the house of James, brother of Jesus (Acts 21:18). Paul sent greetings to at least three churches, to the church meeting in the house of Aquila and Priscilla (Romans 16:5); to the church meeting in the house of Nymphas (Colossians 4:15); to the church meeting in the house of Philemon at Colossae(Philemon 2).

The term church also has a wider meaning. It denotes the whole body of believers, "how that beyond measure I persecuted the church of God, and wasted it" (Galatians 1:13; 1 Corinthians 15:9).

There is an actual, visible, earthly company which is addressed as "the people of God," the "body of Christ."

"It is surely a fact of inexhaustible significance that what our Lord left behind him was not a book, nor a creed, nor a system of thought, nor a rule of life, but a visible community. . . . It was not that a community gathered round an idea, so that the idea was primary and the community secondary. It was that a community called together by the deliberate choice of the Lord himself, and re-created in him. . . ."[2]

2. The Nature of a Church

In Matthew 16:18 Jesus said, "And I say also unto thee, That thou art Peter, and upon this rock I will build my church."

What did Jesus mean by the use of the word "church"?

Jesus certainly meant more than the disciples were able to understand at the time he was speaking. Jesus was telling his disciples that on the basis of that divinely transformed type of character, which is the outgrowth of that faith in deity and messiahship of Jesus expressed by Peter's confession, it

[2] Lesslie Newbigin, *The Household of God,* pp. 20, 21.

was his purpose to build a new congregation, distinct from the old congregation of Israel.

"That would indicate to the disciples that the agency through which their Lord would promote his cause would not be the historical nation of Israel, but a body of people who confessed him as Saviour and Lord." [3]

Later Simon Peter explained this new congregation of people this way:

"But ye are a chosen generation, a royal priesthood, an holy nation, a peculiar people; . . . Which in time past were not a people, but are now the people of God" (1 Peter 2:9, 10).

It is the gathering together of these people of God redeemed by Christ that signified the use of the word "church." The believers referred to as "they" in Acts 2:42, 46 later become identified as the church (Acts 2:47). Those believers had received the words of salvation, were baptized, and continued stedfastly in the apostles' doctrine and fellowship, and in breaking of bread, and in prayers (Acts 2:41, 42).

The nature of the church is evident from the nature of the membership. As the nature of a Christian is to be like Christ so the church is to reflect the nature and work of Christ on earth.

a. *Children of God*

Jesus taught that man must have a new birth before he could be a child of God (John 3:1-6). This birth into the family of God was the result of divine power through personal faith and repentance in Jesus Christ. In John 1:12, 13 we read, "But as many as received him (Christ), to them gave he power to become the sons of God, even to them that believe on his name: Which were born, not of blood, nor of the will of the flesh, nor of the will of man, but of God."

---

[3] H. E. Dana, *Christ's Ecclesia,* pp. 34, 35.

This acceptance into the household of God was described by Paul as an adoption and as a joint heir or son with Jesus. "For as many as are led by the Spirit of God, they are the sons of God. For ye have not received the spirit of bondage again to fear; but ye have received the spirit of adoption, whereby we cry, Abba, Father. The Spirit itself beareth witness with our spirit, that we are the children of God: and if children, then heirs; heirs of God, and joint-heirs with Christ" (Romans 8:14-17).

The children of God have a new nature. They are no longer sons of Adam or the children of darkness. By their nature they seek to be like Christ and carry out his work on earth. Paul speaks of the believers of God. (Ephesians 2:19). The same idea of a family prevails in Galatians 6:10 where Paul writes of the household of faith. God's children are to be together as his family. The nature of a church reflects the coming together of God's children.

b. *Fellowship of Believers*

The Christians are not only sons of God, but they are brothers in Christ. This kinship of one Christian with another is often designated by the word "fellowship."

The Greek word *koinonia* which we translate fellowship means more in the Christian sense than having a good time with family and friends. *Koinonia* is used to express the bond of fellowship that unites Christians. The word describes Christians who share in a common life. It is an inner relationship of people who have been transformed into a new life through God's spirit. The basic ingredient in this fellowship is love. It is a love that was expressed by God in the giving of his son for salvation of man. "Herein is love, not that we loved God, but that he loved us, and sent his Son to be the propitiation for our sins. Beloved, if God so loved us, we ought also to love one another" (1 John 4:10, 11).

This love for Christ and for fellow Christians is necessary if a church is to do its work well. There was a time when church members addressed one another, using the prefix "brother." There are still some pastors who use the terms "Brother John" and "Sister Smith" in identifying or talking with church members.

Love should be a unifying force in church membership. The decisions, plans, and work of a church should carry with them a desire and commitment by each member. In this way the objectives and plans of the church become those of each member.

In the early days of Christianity, the Christians were characterized as ". . . continued stedfastly in the apostles' doctrine and fellowship, and in breaking of bread, and in prayers" (Acts 2:42).

Fellowship was essential for the early Christians. It also is vital to the life of a church today.

c. *A Divine Organism*

The church was created by God through the redemption of people in Jesus Christ. Paul made this fact explicit in speaking to the pastors of Ephesus. "Take heed therefore unto yourselves, and to all the flock, over the which the Holy Ghost hath made you overseers, to feed the church of God, which he hath purchased with his own blood" (Acts 20:28). "A man must belong to Christ first and to the church as a result of belonging to him." [4]

Only those who are redeemed through Christ can be a member of the church. In this sense the church is divine and spiritual. It is not man-made nor dependent upon man for life or direction.

The life of the Christian is life in Christ. At the same time the life of the Christian is the life of Christ in the believer. The Christian has died with Christ and his life is hid

[4] W. T. Conner, *The Gospel of Redemption,* p. 273.

with Christ in God (Colossians 3:3). He is crucified with Christ and now Christ lives in him (Galatians 2:20). He has put off his old self and has put on the new made in the image of the creator (Colossians 3:9, 10). Christians were made dead to the law through the body of Christ, that they should be joined one to another and to him who was raised from the dead (Romans 7:4). The Christian could not exist for one second apart from Christ.

As an organism, Christ is the head. He exercises his rule through his only vicar, the Holy Spirit. The church is Christ's body, a living organism.

d. *Body of Christ*

As a spiritual body the church shares a spiritual union and fellowship with the living Christ.

The church embodies the life of Christ and seeks to manifest that life to all mankind. Christ is the head of the body, the church (Ephesians 1:22; 4:15; Colossians 1:18). It is the business of the body to obey the head. Whatever the head wants is the desire of the body. Christ is the light of the world (John 8:12), so are his people the light of the world (Matthew 5:14).

In 1 Corinthians, chapters 12-14, Paul discusses spiritual gifts in relationship to the church as the body of Christ. He shows that every gift and work performed by members of the body should be for the upbuilding of Christ on earth.

Just as a physical body has many parts, so the congregation of God's people is a body with many parts. These parts are individual members of the congregation.

The hand, the eye, the foot, and other parts of the human body have separate and distinct functions. Yet each member serves the human body in accordance with the mind and will of the head. They serve for a single purpose, to obey the will of the head.

All of the members of Christ's body have gifts and abilities which the church needs to use to fulfill its work on earth. The members of the church serve to carry out the will and purpose of Christ, the head of the body.

3. Mission of a Church

The church receives its mission or purpose from its Lord. Since Christ is the head, then the mission of the church is to do the will of Christ on earth.

There is no place in the New Testament where the exact mission of the church is set forth. However, the Bible says that Christ spoke to his disciples and gave them their mission for life. In speaking to his disciples Jesus was speaking to his church.

There are five references of Jesus speaking to his assembled believers (Matthew 28:18-30; Mark 16:15; Luke 24:47; John 20:21; Acts 1:8). These words have often been referred to as the Great Commission.

a. *The Sphere of the Mission*

". . . and ye shall be witnesses unto me both in Jerusalem, and in all Judea, and in Samaria, and unto the uttermost part of the earth: (Acts 1:8). There was no question about the geographic boundary of the church's witness. In Matthew 28:19 Jesus expressed the sphere as "all nations."

This means the church must penetrate every section of the globe by every possible means with the message that Jesus is Lord. This understanding cannot be restricted to a concept of "foreign missions." It is the church's total mission to go unto all the world.

b. *The Purpose of the Mission*

"Go ye therefore, and teach (make disciples of) all nations, baptizing them in the name of the Father, and of the

Son, and of the Holy Ghost: Teaching them to observe all things whatsoever I have commanded you: and, lo, I am with you alway, even unto the end of the world" (Matthew 28:19, 20).

The church was to lead men to God through Christ and to teach them all the things that Christ taught. This is the changeless purpose or mission of every church regardless of size or location.

A church fulfills its mission or purpose in accordance with its nature. Thus, the nature and purpose of the church determine its functions. "Functions are determined by nature." [5]

The functions of a church indicate what God has ordained or expects his church to do on earth.

B. THE FUNCTIONS OF A CHURCH

The church finds its scope of work in the will of God. Whatever the Lord says for his church to do must be done. These actions become the functions of the church.

The nature of the functions will always be in keeping with the divine nature of a church. Function is a basic kind of action which is consistent with the nature of the church.

"The function of the church must be defined in the light of the plan of Jesus and of the fact of the mediation of the individual Christian between the Saviour and the lost world. The church thus becomes the agency of saved people for enabling them to grow in grace and in the knowledge of our Lord and Saviour, Jesus Christ; and, combining with one another most effectively to bear witness to salvation in the most extensive measure possible." [6]

This work of a church is grouped under five basic functions—to worship, to witness, to educate, to minister, and to apply. These functions are not independent of one

[5] *Ibid.*, p. 276.
[6] W. O. Carver, *The Furtherance of the Gospel*, p. 57.

another, nor are they done in sequence. Instead, they are inter-dependent and inter-related.

The pumping of the blood to every part of the human body is essential for existence. Yet the heart is dependent on the proper digestion of food for its survival.

The effectiveness of a church is dependent on the total performance of its functions. A weakness in worship will reflect itself in witnessing, educating, applying, and ministering. These functions are bound together like the nerves, muscles, veins, and organs of a human body.

1. Explanation of the Functions

a. *To Worship*

To worship is to be aware of God. Worship includes the outgoing of the soul in response to God's revelation of himself to Christians. Paul indicates that when an unbeliever comes into a church dominated by the Spirit, the secrets of his heart will be made manifest (to him) and he will fall down and worship God (1 Corinthians 14:25). In worship Christians find out what God is saying to the church and what the church is committing to God. True worship will find expression in service.

"Worship may involve enjoyment, instruction, plans for action—in fact, true worship will almost inevitably include these—but it is more and other than these. That which transforms these into worship is the fact of God, and the relationship of the worshipers to him. The joy of the worshiper is in God. His instruction is in the will of God. His plans for action are to make God's will prevail in human affairs." [7]

b. *To Witness*

The early days of the New Testament churches were characterized by the witness of Christians that Jesus was alive

[7] Donald G. Miller, *The Nature and Mission of the Church,* p. 104.

and the Saviour of the world. When the witnessing boldness of the apostles Peter and John brought them before the Jerusalem council they had but these words of testimony, "For we cannot but speak the things which we have seen and heard" (Acts 4:20).

Driven from Jerusalem, the persecuted Christians went to the people with their witness instead of waiting for the people to come and hear.

Jesus said, "Ye shall be witnesses unto me" (Acts 1:18).

Though the methods have changed, the function remains the same. The church must bear witness to Jesus Christ. The unsaved person must be confronted with the message of redemption through Christ Jesus.

c. *To Educate*

In setting forth the requirements of a bishop (overseer) Paul said he must be "apt to teach" (1 Timothy 3:2). Paul and Barnabas spent time in Antioch "teaching and preaching the word of the Lord" (Acts 15:35). Teaching and training were necessary to the life of the early church. Converts coming from a pagan world into a Christian community needed instruction for growth and maturity. The pastor of a church was responsible for teaching these new converts. Thus Paul said he should be "apt to teach."

So necessary was Christian education to the life of the church that one of the gifts of the Holy Spirit to the church was that of teachers (Ephesians 4:11).

The epistles Paul wrote to the churches were documents for teaching the Christians in their faith and personal maturity. The epistle of 1 Corinthians was Paul's personal instructions for solving many of the problems that confronted the church at Corinth.

The church by its nature must educate its members in the Christian life and work.

d. *To Minister*

Since the church is Christ's body, the whole church is his ministering body. Yet any member of the church may minister even as any member of a body may proclaim or worship. To minister is to respond to the needs of persons in the name of Christ. Therefore, Christian ministry is the ministry of God's people to human needs.

Jesus set the example for ministering to the needs of others. He said, ". . . the Son of man came not to be ministered unto, but to minister, and to give his life a ransom for many" (Matthew 20:28). The ministry of Christ revealed the depths of the self-giving love of God. The risen Lord continues his ministry through the church, the people of God, the body of Christ.

Though the church is primarily interested in reconciling God and man, this reconciliation vitally affects the relations between man and man.

In Peter's epistle, ministry is expressed as a basic law of the life of Christians and of a congregation. "As every man hath received the gift, even so minister the same one to another, as good stewards of the manifold grace of God" (1 Peter 4:10). From these verses it appears that the root of ministry is love.

e. *To Apply*

Apply in this context means the practical application of Christian principles in all the issues of everyday life.

The concept shoots full of holes the picture of an active, participating Christian as a person who becomes highly involved in Christ-centered activities on Sunday but fails to express them in decisions he makes the rest of the week.

This function has been described in several ways. Some examples are faith and action, word and deed, and belief and behavior. James 1:22 expresses it this way: "Be ye doers of the Word and not hearers only."

When does the effective application of Christian principles take place?

As starters, there's the market place, the home, the office, the polling booth, the golf course, the service club, and in all other interpersonal relationships.

2. Implementation of the Functions

A church plans its work in keeping with its objective. While church objectives have been stated many ways at various times, here is how the Southern Baptist Convention in 1967 identified the objective of a church:

"The objective of a church, composed of baptized believers who share a personal commitment to Jesus Christ as Saviour and Lord, is to be a redemptive body in Christ, through the power of the Holy Spirit, growing toward Christian maturity through worship, witness, education, and ministry, proclaiming the gospel to the whole world, and applying Christian principles to man and society that God's purposes may be achieved."

Once a church has determined what God wants done, the people begin working toward that end.

One of the church's first decisions is to decide how it wants to perform its functions to reach its objective.

A general study of a church will reveal there are at least nine basic continuing activities of primary importance in moving a church toward its objective. These tasks are:

- Govern the life and work of the church under the lordship of Christ.
- Engage in a fellowship of worship, witness, education, ministry, and application.
- Participate in cooperative work with other churches.

- Establish and maintain relationship with various publics.
- Provide resources for the work of the church.
- Teach persons the meaning(s) and skill for Christian living and church membership, using the Bible as the primary source.
- Train church members to perform the tasks of the church.
- Proclaim the gospel to believers and unbelievers.
- Reach persons for Christ and church membership.

Since these tasks belong to the body of believers, the decision for assigning these basic continuing activities belongs to the congregation.

For good administration related tasks are grouped together and assigned to programs within the church to perform.

Southern Baptist churches have discovered that work is accomplished when people are grouped together into units and then given assigned responsibilities. These units of work are called organizations. Examples are Brotherhood, Sunday School, and Training Union.

Those working units in a church which are given specific tasks to accomplish through a structured approach to learning are called church program organizations.

3. Brotherhood Program

Brotherhood is a church program organization for involving all men and boys in a church in missions. Other church program organizations are Sunday School, Training Union, Woman's Missionary Union, and Music Ministry.

The Southern Baptist Convention gave the mission dimension to the Brotherhood in its annual meeting in June, 1965 when it approved the following objective for the Brotherhood Commission:

"The Brotherhood Commission is to support the Southern Baptist Convention in its tasks of bringing men to God through Christ by fostering programs that will assist the churches in their task of leading men, young men, and boys to a deeper commitment to missions, to a more meaningful prayer life for missions, to a larger stewardship on behalf of missions, and to a personal involvement in missions."

In adopting this objective, Southern Baptist churches identified a need and a means for meeting this need. The need was for men and boys to have a mission program. This need was in keeping with the nature of a church to fulfill its responsibility of "teaching them to observe all things whatsoever I have commanded you" (Matthew 28:20). The means for meeting this need is the Brotherhood program.

a. *Objective*

The objective of Brotherhood in a Baptist church is to support the church in its task of bringing men and boys to God through Christ by leading them to a deeper commitment to missions, to a more meaningful prayer life for missions, to a larger stewardship on behalf of missions, and to a personal involvement in missions.

This objective relates to the nature and mission of a church. The New Testament teaches that a church is a body of baptized believers, in covenant with God and each other, for the presenting of the gospel of Jesus Christ to all people of the world with the purpose of leading them to personal faith in Christ and obedience to his will. Such a definition embodies the mission of a church.

Missions is what the church is and does to achieve its mission in all areas of human need which are on the growing edge of the church's confrontation with the non-Christian world.

For men and boys, missions is extending the gospel

beyond the immediate congregation. While the Sunday School is reaching prospects for the church, the Brotherhood will be reaching people of unusual circumstance and those beyond the normal reach of the congregation. To accomplish this purpose, the Brotherhood involves men, and boys in mission study and action.

b. *Tasks*

The Brotherhood fulfills four tasks for a church. They are (1) teach missions; (2) engage in mission action; (3) support world missions through praying and giving, and (4) provide and interpret information regarding the work of the church and the denomination.

The next four chapters explain these tasks in detail.

2. Teaching Missions

CHAPTER OUTLINE

A. RELATIONSHIP OF TEACHING TO LEARNING

B. THE IMPORTANCE OF TEACHING MISSIONS

1. Helps the Church Fulfill Its Responsibility in Teaching Missions
2. Helps Persons to Know What God Is Doing in the World
3. Deepens Faith of Men and Boys

C. THE CONTENT FOR TEACHING MISSIONS

1. The Missionary Message of the Bible
2. The Role of the Church in Missions
3. Progress of Christian Missions
4. Contemporary Missions

D. LEARNING OPPORTUNITIES IN MISSIONS

1. At Regular Meetings
2. At Special Times

E. RELATIONSHIPS IN TEACHING MISSIONS

1. Brotherhood and Sunday School
2. Brotherhood and Training Union
3. Brotherhood and Woman's Missionary Union
4. Brotherhood and the Music Ministry

• The basic task a church assigns to Brotherhood is to teach missions to men, and boys. This task is foundational to all of the experiences of Brotherhood.

To teach missions means to lead persons to develop new concepts, understandings, and appreciations of the total mission of the church; to develop new attitudes about the mission of the church and the persons not now enrolled in its programs; and to develop new skills through taking part in the church's mission.

Jesus was a great teacher during his ministry on earth. The Bible is full of accounts of how he used every opportunity to teach his message. There are numerous accounts of Jesus teaching in the synagogues. The synagogue was the center of religious thought and Jesus was teaching religious truth. The importance that Jesus placed on teaching made the synagogue the logical place to teach the people.

Jesus taught in preparing his disciples for their work. The words of Jesus, often described as the Sermon on the Mount, were directed to his disciples: "And seeing the multitudes, he went up into a mountain: and when he was set, his disciples came unto him: And he opened his mouth, and taught them" (Matthew 5:1, 2).

The great invitation of Jesus in Matthew 11:29 was, "Take my yoke upon you, and learn of me; . ." This was learning by example and experience.

Jesus indicates that every Christian is a learner. The church fulfills its function, to educate, when the members learn the message, meaning, and work of Christ.

A teaching church will provide a complete educational program for its members. This includes teaching the biblical revelation, Christian theology, Christian ethics, Christian history, Baptist polity and organization, music, and missions. Through study in all of these areas the church members are able to understand their faith better and to learn more about God's will for their lives.

The Brotherhood assignment to teach missions to men, and boys is a significant part of a church's well-rounded teaching ministry.

In teaching missions the Brotherhood leads its members to a growing awareness of the nature and implication of God's missionary purpose in the world. At the same time the individual is given an opportunity to respond to God's purpose through personal commitment and obedience. This learning experience should continue throughout the life span of a Christian.

Every Christan is expected to seek to learn more about God's work and how his own life can be effectively used for God. The psalmist said, "The entrance of thy words giveth light; it giveth understanding unto the simple" (Psalm 119:130). Through study the Christian comes to a personal understanding of his own mission for God in the world.

A. RELATIONSHIP OF TEACHING TO LEARNING

The church uses leaders to make its curriculum plan a learning experience for persons. The curriculum plan encompasses facts and concepts persons learn and actions they can do.

Learning is acquiring knowledge or skill designed to bring about changes in the lives of learners as they relate to God and other people. Teaching, on the other hand, is planning for and guiding the learning experiences which will bring about the desired changes. Education describes the teaching-learning process.

The Brotherhood program is concerned with the teacher and learner. The Brotherhood program begins with a boy in the first grade and continues to provide him in missions throughout adult life. As learning about missions takes place, the individual matures through changes in knowledge, understanding, attitudes, and skills.

A learner gives evidence of change as he masters the basic study material. Understandings are the personal meanings the learner perceives from his knowledge. Attitudes are the learner's feelings and response to what is being learned. Skills involve the ability to use one's knowledge effectively.

Men and boys universally need to know more about the world they live in and God's purpose for it. The lack of adequate information brings about a breakdown in understanding the personal implications for serving God. A byproduct of this information vacuum is a wrong attitude toward peoples of the world which greatly impairs mission work.

The Brotherhood program in a church seeks to solve this problem by cultivating in men, young men, and boys "(1) a Christlike concern for all people, (2) an intimate knowledge of how the Christian fellowship is being extended at home and abroad, and (3) a hearty participation in all efforts to enlarge this fellowship of Christian faith until it covers the earth." [1]

Through teaching the knowledge that relates to God's redemptive plans for the world the Brotherhood will lead its members to have compassion for the people of the world. Such inward feelings will develop the proper attitudes for participation in missions.

There is one other relationship of teaching to learning for the Christian. This involves the Holy Spirit. God speaks to the believer through his Spirit. A study of the word and work of God provides the Holy Spirit an opportunity to speak to the learner.

[1] Nevin D. Harner and David D. Baker, *Missionary Education in Your Church*, p. 19.

Paul told the Christians in Corinth, "But God hath revealed them unto us by his Spirit: for the Spirit searcheth all things, yea, the deep things of God" (1 Corinthians 2:10).

B. THE IMPORTANCE OF TEACHING MISSIONS

Southern Baptist churches had no comprehensive Bible-based curriculum for teaching missions to men, young men, and boys until its action in June, 1965, establishing the following objective of the Brotherhood Commission:

> The objective of the Brotherhood Commission is to support the Southern Baptist Convention in its task of bringing men to God through Christ by fostering programs that will assist the churches in their tasks of leading men, young men, and boys to a deeper commitment to missions, to a more meaningful prayer life for missions, to a larger stewardship on behalf of missions, and to a personal involvement in missions.

This objective requires a mission study program that is Bible-based, church-oriented, and action-inducing. This need for mature understandings of missions is important for several reasons.

1. Helps the Church Fulfill Its Responsibility in Teaching Missions

Until the Convention's action the churches had no correlated missions program for men. Yet the church was commanded by Christ to teach "them to observe all things whatsoever I have commanded you."

Through Brotherhood and Woman's Missionary Union, a church can now provide the necessary mission information and activities for all of its members.

2. Helps Persons to Know What God Is Doing in the World

God's work in the world is personalized through instructions in missions. It is not enough to know what God is doing in the church community; the vision must be increased to the distant horizons of the world. Where the individual has been busy on a half acre, he must now become engaged in world conquest.

God is concerned about the whole world. John 3:16 says, "For God so loved the world." It was for the world and its needs that Jesus died. It was the world that Jesus thought of when he gave the Great Commission to his disciples.

A study of missions will reveal what God has been doing in the world and wants to accomplish. Motivation and participation can grow out of this study of need.

3. Deepens Faith of Men and Boys

As individuals study missions, varied results occur.

In boys such a study will lay a foundation for Christian growth. Through an understanding of missions, boys learn to give of themselves in service for others. In coming to this understanding at an early age boys will develop attitudes and convictions that continue on into manhood.

Mission study offers to men insights into world events that require a deep personal faith. Young men are faced with the primary decision of deciding about life's vocation. World events and world needs play a vital role in this decision.

A study of missions will quicken an individual's understanding of personal responsibility. Missions involves an organized and individual effort. Each victory or defeat in world missions can help deepen a person's faith.

C. THE CONTENT FOR TEACHING MISSIONS

In teaching missions Brotherhood centers its study on the missionary message of the Bible, emphasizing strongly the role of the church in missions. Learners also study the progress of Christian missions and contemporary missions.

1. The Missionary Message of the Bible

The Bible is the account of God's work in redeeming a lost world. The opening chapters of the Bible reveal a world of God's creation. The crowning glory of God's handiwork was the creation of Adam and Eve. At first there was communion between God and his created beings, man and woman. Then sin separated God from man. Sin had to be judged and punished, but God continued to seek man and restore him to communion and fellowship.

The Bible gives the account of God's concern and witness to the unredeemed. Abram was called to be the father of a chosen people. These chosen people were called Israel and became God's witness to the nations of the world. The Old Testament is a record of the chosen people and their witness of the true God. Mighty prophets were raised up to speak God's message to the people of Israel.

Ultimately, God sent his Son into the world to call the world to repentance and salvation. Jesus willingly gave himself as a sacrifice and atonement for man's sins. It was the risen Christ that gave a commission to his followers to bear witness to salvation through his death to all of the people of the world.

To assist the believers in telling the message, Christ promised and gave the Holy Spirit. The Holy Spirit came upon the believers in an upper room on the day of Pentecost with remarkable power. The believers went into the streets of Jerusalem and began to witness to all people with amazing results. More than 3,000 people accepted Christ as their Saviour and Lord.

The Holy Spirit continued to guide and strengthen the efforts of the early Christians. It was the Holy Spirit that directed Philip to speak to a man from Ethiopia and that led Simon Peter to the home of Cornelius, a Gentile. Peter described the incident this way: "The Spirit bade me go with them, nothing doubting" (Acts 11:12).

The first missionaries, Paul and Barnabas, were sent out by the church at Antioch under the direction of the Holy Spirit. Paul, the great apostle, missionary, letter writer, and Christian statesman was guided, comforted, and ministered to by the Holy Spirit.

The gift of the Spirit is another evidence of God's concern for people. This same Spirit works today in the lives of Christians.

The Bible contains a revelation of God's redemptive concern for man and a record of man's attempt to fulfill God's commission of witnessing to the world.

2. The Role of the Church in Missions

The biblical account of the people who believed on the day of Pentecost states: "Then they that gladly received his word were baptized . . . And they continued stedfastly in the apostles' doctrine and fellowship, and in breaking of bread, and in prayers . . . Praising God, and having favour with all the people. And the Lord added to the church daily such as should be saved" (Acts 2:41, 42, 47). These believers assembled themselves together and became known as "the church." From this early reference the church became more prominent in missions.

The church is the heart or hub of all mission work. Apostle Paul said repeatedly the church is "the body of Christ" (Ephesians 4:12). As the body of Christ the church is seeking to continue Christ's mission upon the earth. To be a member of today's church involves each member in what Christ is doing in the world.

It is the church that involves itself in finding out what Christ, the head of the church, wants to accomplish in the world.

The membership of a church is composed of God's children. Those who belong to God are eager to carry out God's command for reaching people. Such a desire is fulfilled as individuals and as members of the body of Christ.

The mission of a church is to present the gospel of Jesus Christ to all of the people of the world, both at home and abroad, with the purpose of leading them to personal faith in Christ and obedience to his will.

Emil Brunner states, "The church exists by mission just as a fire exists by burning. Where there is no mission, there is no church: and where there is neither church nor mission, there is no faith."

The church has a mission to the world. It is not fulfilled through a few individuals performing a few mission projects. The church's mission is accomplished through the entire church understanding and performing its responsibility.

Dr. Hugo Culpepper, director of missions for the Home Mission Board, states:

"It is difficult to bring even keen and instructed church members to the point of seeing that the church's life and witness, her encounter with the world and therefore her place of obedience, is precisely in the work of her lay members Monday through Saturday. Sunday, it should be understood, is the day on which the church makes a necessary withdrawal from its engagement with the world to renew inner springs of the divine life within her through worship.

"This deep and disastrous distortion in the church's life has its roots so far back in history that it's very hard for the churches to recognize it for what it is. But one may safely say that the church will not share the one gospel with the whole world until the churches undergo a deep repentance at this point and learn again that the church is the mission."

As a program of the church, Brotherhood guides men and boys in an understanding of the church as God's mission.

3. The Progress of Christian Missions

The mission cause became a world movement with the command of Jesus (Matthew 28:19, 20). The Christians of the first three centuries were committed to missions. When the Jerusalem Christians were scattered because of persecution, "they went everywhere preaching the word." Commercial travelers, soldiers, sailors, and businessmen also helped spread Christianity. Small groups of believers banded together in many countries. In the face of persecutions Christianity still made inroads into paganism.

In the Middle Ages (A.D.500 - A.D.1450) the church lost some of its mission zeal. There was a tendency to dwell on an institutional type of religion. James Smart documents this fact in *The Teaching Ministry of the Church.*

During the Reformation period (16th Century) churches made limited response to their missionary responsibility. There was little advance in missions other than the migration of Christians to North America.

By 1700, interest in missions began to increase. The modern missionary movement was inaugurated in 1793 when the London Missionary Society sent William Carey to India. In 1812 Adoniram Judson and Luther Rice sailed from America to India. Though they went as missionaries from the Congregational church, they later became Baptists.

Judson later went to Burma while Rice returned to America to raise money for the support of Judson and his work. The appeals of Rice to the Baptist churches on the Atlantic coast helped to waken the churches to their mission responsibilities.

The progress of Christian missions include the origin, development, and progress of Southern Baptist foreign, home, state, and associational missions.

In keeping with the teachings of the New Testament, Southern Baptists center their work in each church because each church has its own mission to fulfill.

Although each church is committed to its own work, there are times when churches cooperate in performing certain mission responsibilities.

When several Baptist churches work together on a common project in a small geographic area, that is identified as associational missions. The cooperative work of the churches in a state is state missions. Home missions is the cooperative work of churches in an area encompassing all of the states, Panama, Cuba, and Puerto Rico. That work done outside the United States and its territories under the cooperative auspices of churches is foreign missions. All of this work is known as Southern Baptist mission work.

The Brotherhood develops its study material in close relationship with the Home Mission Board and Foreign Mission Board and with appropriate emphasis on state and associational missions.

4. Contemporary Missions

A study of contemporary missions includes the current world context in which mission work is done, the philosophy of Christian missions, Southern Baptist mission strategy and work, and the mission work of other Christian and non-Christian groups.

To understand mission philosophy and strategy, church members need to know the setting in which mission work is done. World context refers to the geographical, political, cultural, sociological, and economic background of a given area.

The philosophy of Christian missions explores the purpose or motivation for outreach. Mission strategy involves technique and procedure in outreach. A study of Baptist mission work involves an examination of what is being done in a given area.

Study of the mission work of other Christian or non-Christian groups helps Baptists see other ways to communicate the gospel of Christ and to evaluate these approaches.

A major emphasis in contemporary missions is placed upon church support of representative missions through prayer, finances, and personnel. Tithing is cited as the biblical concept underlying mission support. The church budget, Cooperative Program, and special offerings are channels of the financial support of mission work.

D. LEARNING OPPORTUNITIES IN MISSIONS

Learning takes place in many ways amid various circumstances. The Brotherhood program in a church emphasizes flexibility in its efforts to meet the need for mission study. Here are several ways:

1. At Regular Meetings

The basic plan for teaching missions is through the use of a dated curriculum at regular meetings of the organizational units. This curriculum plan is found in *Baptist Men's Journal* and *Guide* for men and *Crusader, Crusader Counselor, Probe* and *Probe* (*Leadership Edition*) for boys.

This curriculum plan composes the monthly study and action program for men and young men and the weekly study and action program for boys.

Every man, young man, and boy should receive appropriate reading materials to get the full benefit of this curriculum plan.

Publication	Baptist Men	Officers of Baptist Men	Crusaders	Crusader Counselor	Pioneers	Pioneer Counselors	RA Leader and Committee	Brotherhood Director
Brotherhood Builder							X	X
Baptist Men's Journal	X	X						
Guide		X						
Crusader			X	X				
Crusader Counselor				X				
Probe					X	X		
Probe (Leadership Edition)						X		

Developed with continuity, balance and sequence in mind, the curriculum plan is Bible-based, church oriented, and action-inducing.

2. At Special Times

Books on missions are available for men and boys wanting to enlarge their understanding of missions beyond the basic curriculum plan.

Mission study books are provided annually by the Home Mission Board and Foreign Mission Board on interesting areas of mission work. Also available are books in the mission action series, and seminary extension studies in missions.

They may be studied, individually, in special classes, and in large Brotherhood groups. The setting may be a classroom, a seminar or a retreat.

In most churches the study of books on home and foreign missions is part of a mission emphasis which includes prayer for home and foreign missions.

Periodically, churches also participate in world mission conferences, usually through the association. A world mission conference includes the study of a mission book and messages by missionaries.

The study of missions is one part of the total curriculum plan of Southern Baptist churches. Woman's Missionary Union and Brotherhood serve the church by teaching missions. Other content areas important in the spiritual growth of church members are developed in Sunday School, Training Union, and Music Ministry. In churches with one curriculum plan it is important for all study to be planned in proper relationship.

Below are church program organizations and the content areas where they provide study.

ORGANIZATION	CURRICULUM AREA
Sunday School	Biblical Revelation
Brotherhood	Missions
Woman's Missionary Union	
Training Union	Christian Theology Christian History Christian Ethics Church Polity and Organization
Music Ministry	Music and Hymnody

While each of the program organizations has a distinctive content area, proper relationships can bring about a balanced, comprehensive study program in a church.

1. Brotherhood and Sunday School

In Sunday School, instruction in the biblical revelation leads members in a study of God's disclosure of himself and his will for man as revealed through the Scriptures. Such a study provides the basis for missions. The more profound one's knowledge of the biblical revelation becomes, the clearer one's sense of missionary responsibility becomes. The study of missions begins with the Bible. Through the Brotherhood program men and boys are led into a specialized study of the missionary message of the Bible.

A study of the biblical revelation brings into focus the church's and individual's responsibility in mission activities.

2. Brotherhood and Training Union

Training Union has five study areas, each related to missions.

The Training Union study of Christian history reflects the advances and triumphs of churches in fulfilling their mission. While the study program of Christian history in Training Union gives the broad historical base, the study of missions derives benefits for understanding the plans and methods of contemporary missions.

In Christian theology, Training Union members study the Bible to discover the need for Christians to engage in missions. Through theology the character and purpose of God, the nature of man, and God's redemptive plans for man come into sharp focus. These basic doctrines further accent the compulsion of missions.

The study of church polity and organization in Training Union brings understanding of the ways people are related together to accomplish God's work through their church and denomination.

The study of Christian ethics is a study of the application of Christian principles as revealed in the Bible. Christian missions and man's relationship with man go hand in hand. The study of ethics undergirds the mission effort. A proper grasp of Christian ethics is important to the Brotherhood's study of missions.

3. Brotherhood and Woman's Missionary Union

Brotherhood and Woman's Missionary Union have a vital relationship in the study of missions. These two organizations share a common task of teaching missions in the church. Although the content areas are the same, the audience, approaches, and methods are different. Where there is value, joint planning and joint study are suggested. The

Brotherhood and WMU provide the means for a church to reach its entire membership in mission study.

4. Brotherhood and the Music Ministry

Music is a part of all programs in a church. The study of hymnody carries deep mission concepts. Music affords many people an opportunity to sing the message of Christ. Music is both a means of strengthening the Christian's life and extending the Christian message. Music is a contributor to all mission work.

The study of missions is one area of the church's total teaching program. It is a part of the whole. So much so that when a church omits missions it has cut out a significant part of its life. The total curriculum allows a church to offer its members a balanced and comprehensive approach to Bible study.

3. Engaging in Mission Action

CHAPTER OUTLINE

A. CONCEPT OF MISSION ACTION

1. Biblical Foundations
2. Meaning of Mission Action
3. Scope of Mission Action

B. PROGRAM OF MISSION ACTION

1. Discovering Needs
2. Selecting Needs
3. Assigning Responsibility
4. Conducting Mission Action

C. RELATIONSHIPS

1. To Woman's Missionary Union
2. To Other Church Program Organizations
3. To the Church Mission Committee
4. To the Associational Brotherhood Program
5. To Community and Government Programs

A. CONCEPT OF MISSION ACTION

1. Biblical Foundations

A Christian has the obligation to minister and witness. Jesus said, "Ye have not chosen me, but I have chosen you, and ordained you, that ye should go and bring forth fruit . . ." (John 15:16). Persons who witness and serve others assist Christ in his saving work.

The nature of a person's salvation compels that believer to give of himself to bear witness to Christ. When the unbeliever is converted and becomes a child of God, compassion for other people grows in his heart. This compassion is motivated by a love for others and a desire to bring them to a conversion experience in Christ.

James wrote, ". . . faith without works is dead" (James 2:20). The response to the coming of the Holy Spirit on Pentecost was a sharing of faith (Acts 2:1-36). When persecution arose, the early believers prayed for courage to witness (Acts 4:29).

A tree is judged by its fruits and not its roots. Yet the roots produce the fruit. The two are interrelated. So it is with faith and works. One is a part of the other.

Paul said in Romans 14:12 that everyone should give an account of himself to God. The stewardship of life indicates God has a priority on all that Christians are and have.

The Christian reaches his highest point of dedication when he learns to deny himself for others. In church membership there is a uniting of individuals in love, worship, service, prayer, witness, fellowship, and other attributes peculiar to God's children.

Each member of a church has his own place of service. Paul uses the picture of the human body to describe this relationship. The human body cannot function properly without the eyes, hands, and the feet. Neither can the church without the service of its members. The hand does not say to the eye, "I have no need of thee." There is a need for the activity of the eye and hand. So it is with the members of the church.

Christ through the Holy Spirit guides Christians in witnessing and ministering. Sometimes the Holy Spirit calls a person to a lifetime of one particular action. At other times the Holy Spirit leads a person to fulfill a particular need. The Holy Spirit may lead in individual or group actions. The Spirit kept Paul from going into Bithynia, yet led Philip on the road to Gaza.

Jesus set the example for Christians to follow in ministering to people. He declared that his mission was one of service to others (Luke 4:18-19; Mark 10:45). In Luke's account Jesus mentioned the poor, brokenhearted, captives, blind, and the bruised. Jesus also showed great compassion for the sick.

In today's society the boy in the parable of the prodigal son would be classified as a delinquent. However, Jesus so related the account that he emphasized the value and sacredness of the boy, "there is joy in the presence of the angels of God over one sinner that repenteth" (Luke 15:1-10).

Jesus made service a significant part of his teachings. He promised that the simplest deed of service would in no wise be unrewarded (Matthew 10:42). He taught that being a neighbor included a deed of service (Luke 10:35-37). He declared that he came to seek and to save the lost. His actions brought condemnation for eating with publicans and sinners.

Jesus was concerned about the needs of people to the

point he gave himself to the neglected, the lost, the crippled, the delinquent, the bereaved, and to all the people that needed love, care, salvation, and hope. Likewise, Christians are under compulsion to discover ways to minister to persons. In so doing they are translating into actions the basic intentions of Jesus.

The service of Christians in behalf of other people should reflect a recognition of the wholeness of the individual. The needs of human beings are varied, but their needs relate to the total person. It follows that the physical, social, mental, and spiritual needs cannot be separated or isolated. To supply adequate food, clothing, and medical care will not meet all the needs of individuals. Helping a person to become a Christian and ignoring his inability to read or hold a job will not meet all of his needs as a person. Jesus helped Zaccheus not only to find salvation, but to find a friend.

Complex problems face Christians today. Most lists would include the slums, the increasing number of alcoholics, the secularization of urban life, the economic disorder from automation, the deterioration of home life, the increased crime rate, the mental breakdown within society, and the unsettled community life. These problems challenge the Christians of today to minister to people in the spirit and love of Christ.

But to meet the challenge of today's world requires maturity, training, experience, and dedication. Take ministering to alcoholics, for example. People addicted to drink need help at many points. They need Christ but they also need something else—help in personal faith and growth. Alcoholism is not easily conquered. Those who perform a ministry to alcoholics must have a particular skill and training.

Not all challenges can be met by individuals. Many of the blights and tensions of the social order require the attention of a group.

The implications in biblical teaching about service to persons in need reemphasize the truth that wherever there is a need, there is Christian duty and opportunity.

2. Meaning of Mission Action

Mission action is the organized effort of a church to minister and witness to persons of special need or circumstance who, without this special effort, are often bypassed in the church's direct outreach activities.

Brotherhood and WMU are the church organizations best equipped to conduct this activity.

Mission action is only one part of a church's effort to carry out Christ's command "to make disciples of all nations."

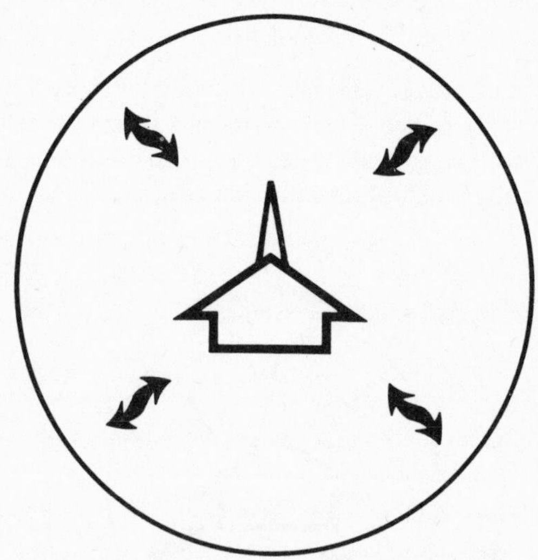

The Sunday School leads in involving church members to reach persons for Christ and church membership. In most churches this means the people in the church community either geographically or socially.

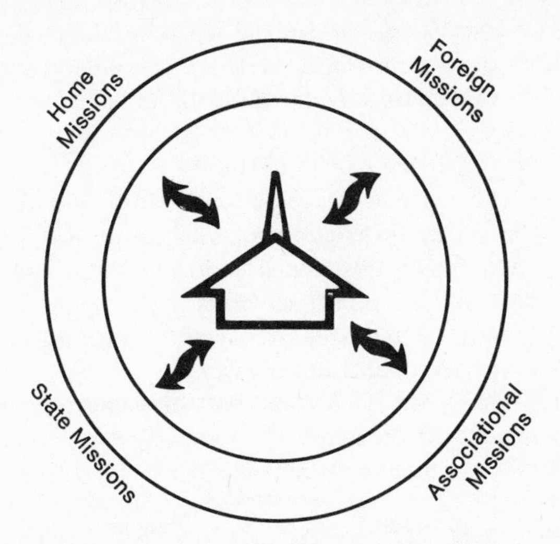

Representative mission programs (those programs which conduct mission work on behalf of many churches in associations, states, and other countries) attempt to reach people through institutional mission efforts.

Between where church outreach activities normally leaves off and representative missions begins live the people who are the target of mission action.

Ideally, every church should attempt to reach every person for Christ and church membership. However, in many cases, barriers exist which limit a church's outreach effort. These barriers are economic, social, educational, racial, or a combination of two or more. They are erected by churches and sometimes by the people themselves. In any case these persons with special needs require a special approach. Hence the need for mission action.

This same need for a witness and ministry exists on foreign mission fields, thus requiring medical, educational, and other specialized approaches.

3. Scope of Mission Action

a. *Geography*

Mission action is one expression of a church's mission program. Its primary intent is the personal involvement of church members in missions work in the area in which the church is located. However, there are no rigid geographical boundaries to mission action. Wherever a church organizes to minister or witness in Christ's name to persons of special need or circumstance, this is mission action.

b. *Types*

The types of mission action vary because the needs of people are different. Just as Jesus was concerned about the blind, the immoral, the crippled, the wealthy, the poor and the downcast, the church must give itself to people with needs. Jesus not only revealed the good news of salvation but he personally demonstrated a love for people.

In like manner, the Brotherhood program in a church seeks to lead men and boys to minister and witness to the people of special need in the community. Examples of individuals and groups whose needs can be met through mission action include:

- Language groups and racial and cultural minorities (Indians, Latin Americans, Orientals, Europeans, Jews, Negroes, international students)
- Physically handicapped (blind, deaf, retarded)
- Socially handicapped (underprivileged, overprivileged, migrants, transients, illiterates, juvenile delinqents, imprisoned, parolees, former prisoners and their families, alcoholics, unwed mothers)
- Persons in institutions (rest homes, hospitals)
- Persons in military service
- Persons in areas where the organization of a church is impossible

While mission action often focuses on persons in target groups, it also encompasses target issues, such as moral problems.

B. A PROGRAM OF MISSION ACTION

1. Discovering Needs

A mission action program is planned on the basis of needs. Needs of persons can be discovered through a mission action survey. Planning and conducting a survey are the responsibilities of the Brotherhood and WMU councils. These organizations may work jointly or independently to see that a survey is efficiently implemented. Coordinating the survey is the work of the church council. The essential tool for planning and conducting the survey is the *Mission Action Survey Guide*.

2. Selecting Needs

On the basis of needs discovered, the Brotherhood director and WMU director work together in making recommendations to the church council regarding which needs should be met and who should meet them. The needs discovered will probably fall into three categories.

Getting the highest priority are those needs which can be met by mission work already established, such as mission centers and rescue missions.

Those needs which community agencies and institutions can meet should receive second priority.

The third level of needs include those which call for establishing and maintaining new ministries.

3. Assigning Responsibility

Once the needs to be met are selected, the church assigns its responsibility for meeting those needs to Brotherhood and WMU together or independently.

4. Conducting Mission Action

Two approaches lend themselves to meeting needs through mission action. They are projects and ongoing activities.

a. *Projects*

Short in duration, projects have a distinguishable beginning and ending time. They often relate to ongoing work.

Boys in the Crusader and Pioneer Divisions of the Brotherhood program favor projects because of their short interest span.

Brotherhood units receive help in conducting mission action projects from their periodicals and the *Mission Action Projects Guide* sold at the Baptist book store.

b. *Ongoing Activities*

Ongoing mission action seeks to meet needs which are more long term or continuous. These needs demand the attention of persons who are willing to minister and witness over a long enough period of time to make a lasting contribution.

Basic guidance materials are mission action group guides for such specialized groups and issues as the sick, poor, illiterate, imprisoned, juvenile delinquent, international student, aged, military, Negro, language group, person in crisis, alcoholic and drug addict, non-evangelical, persons in resort areas, and moral problems.

The process for organizing ongoing activities is for adults and young people to volunteer for work in a mission action group according to their interest and aptitude. The group, headed by a group leader, engages in a continuing cycle of actions for one year or more, depending on the time needed to get effective results. During that period the group will be oriented to their work, survey the need, plan their work, conduct the work, share and evaluate results, and train to improve their work.

Once underway, groups meet monthly at a time convenient to group members, emphasizing training and sharing. Materials to help guide groups in their work are listed in the *Mission Action Group Guides.*

The Brotherhood council plays a major coordination role in the formation of mission action groups. After broad categories of need for mission action have been determined, the formation of groups could follow this process.

(1) Determine Mission Action Groups Needed

This action is performed by the Brotherhood council alone or by the Brotherhood and Woman's Missionary Union councils together.

When groups are formed across organizational lines, the Brotherhood director and WMU director will work out an acceptable plan to administer the work. In most cases the mission action group will be attached to the group which initiated the work. Or, the group may be administered by the organization to which the leader belongs.

For example, a mission action group may be made up of men and women with a man as the leader. The group could be administered by Baptist Men because the group leader would be on the Baptist Men planning committee. In that case, a woman should be appointed assistant group leader to report to the WMS planning group.

(2) Inform and Enlist

Groups are composed of persons who volunteer their services on the basis of their interest and concern for the needs to be met. When the Brotherhood council discovers community needs and determines which needs it will attempt to meet, persons are asked to volunteer to work on a continuing basis in each area of work to be undertaken.

Brotherhood and WMU leaders have the responsibility of publicizing the opportunities for service through mission action. The organizations may work together or separately. Many persons who aren't enrolled in Brotherhood will join a mission action group because of its unusual interest. Brotherhood leaders will want to encourage these persons to participate to the limit of their interest, and not insist that they take part in every phase of Brotherhood work.

The Brotherhood council will coordinate the process of informing church members of mission action opportunities, working with age-level organization leaders to plan the most effective presentation possible.

Among the interesting ways to inform persons about opportunities for service include:

- Presenting needs in the community by testimony or slides
- Using an attractive announcement booklet to outline mission action opportunities
- Conducting a "look-see tour"

- Publicizing in church bulletins accounts of pending mission action opportunities with the request that persons indicate their interests
- Interpreting mission action opportunities at a luncheon or dinner for men of the church, permitting them to volunteer for service.

(3) Determine Groups and Enlist Leaders

The sign-up process is like preregistration. Signing up indicates the number of persons interested. From these interested persons the number of groups needed can be formed. Groups can be small—three to six persons working together. Or there may be as many as 12 to 14 persons in the group.

Baptist Men enlists leaders for its mission action groups. Group leaders serve on the Baptist Men planning committee, coordinating their work with other work in the organization.

(4) Train Leaders and Provide Resources

A single training session can be conducted for all mission action group leaders.

Broad plans for the training session should be made by the Brotherhood council if more than one unit is involved. If all group leaders are from the same unit of Baptist Men, the Baptist Men planning committee will plan this training.

The session should be based on content in the appropriate mission action group guide and *Baptist Men in Missions*. Each group member will need a group guide.

Group leaders need to understand how to get money to do their work. The Brotherhood portion of the church budget will contain it if the Brotherhood has planned wisely. The availability of funds is one reason the church council and congregation should determine what needs will be met. When the church is committed to getting the work done, the church will provide the resources.

(5) Begin Group Action

After all the groundwork has been laid, the group is ready to begin work. A group engages in a cycle of actions based on suggestions in the mission action group guides with help from the section for the Mission Activity Leader in *Guide*. The group leader on the Baptist Men planning committee reports the progress of his group which the Brotherhood council relays to the congregation.

C. RELATIONSHIPS

1. To Woman's Missionary Union

The mission action relationship of Brotherhood and Woman's Missionary Union occurs at four points.

First, both programs have the same task—engage in mission action. Between the two organizations all members of a Baptist church should get the opportunity to participate in mission action.

Second, both programs have the same concept of mission action. Mission action is the church's effort to reach people of special need and/or circumstance.

Third, both programs have the same basic approaches in mission action. This similarity makes it possible for the two organizations to conduct joint mission actions, work separately with the same target group, or work separately with different target groups without conflict.

Fourth, both organizations use the same mission action materials. The basic materials for conducting mission actions are jointly produced by Brotherhood and WMU in cooperation with the Home Mission Board and other appropriate Southern Baptist agencies.

2. To Other Church Program Organizations

a. *Sunday School*

The Brotherhood task of mission action and the Sunday School task of outreach are both efforts of the church to reach people for Christ. The difference is in the target. Both organizations should avoid duplication of efforts by working through the church council.

b. *Training Union*

Training Union's new member orientation prepares new members to take an active role in mission action. Training Union's program of member training equips church members with the basic skills needed to perform the functions of the church.

Brotherhood's program of mission action offers opportunity for men and boys to exercise these skills in reaching persons of special need or circumstance.

Training Union's program of leader training discovers and trains persons in general leadership skills. These newly-trained leaders can find opportunities for service as group leaders in mission action.

Specific training in a mission action area should be provided by Brotherhood or WMU and coordinated through the church council.

c. *Church Music Program*

Individuals or groups who are trained in music can find expression in mission action directed by Brotherhood and WMU. Requests for musical assistance should go to the church music director for coordination.

3. To the Church Missions Committee

The missions committee should provide the leaders for mission work requiring heavy administrative responsibilities in facilities, finances, and employed personnel. The Brotherhood and WMU organizations provide voluntary workers to conduct activities in new and existing missions. Work of the missions committee is coordinated in the church council.

4. To the Associational Brotherhood Program

The associational Brotherhood provides to church Brotherhoods that assistance beyond the capability of the church. That assistance includes mission action. As in individual churches, the associational Brotherhood and Woman's Missionary Union may plan and carry out joint actions as needed. This work is coordinated through the associational council.

5. To Community and Government Programs

The Brotherhood program has a relationship with community agencies and governmental programs which help people of special need or circumstance. Examples are probation courts, detention homes, prisons, homes for the aged, state colleges and universities, aid of poverty programs, services to physically and mentally handicapped, alcoholics, dope addicts, and military veterans.

The purpose of ministering and witnessing to persons in need should underlie this relationship. In no sense does the relationship give the Brotherhood program the right to tell any agency how to do its work.

4. Supporting World Missions Through Prayer and Giving

CHAPTER OUTLINE

A. INTRODUCTION

B. PRAYER

1. Nature
2. Role of Prayer in Missions
3. Opportunities
4. Challenge

C. GIVING

1. Nature
2. Role of Giving in Missions
3. Opportunities

D. SUMMARY

A. INTRODUCTION

Pleas for prayer and more money to meet urgent needs underline letters from Southern Baptist missionaries which pour in from mission fields around the world.

"Only eight men in our village claim to be Christians," a missionary in Alaska wrote. "Others have professed Christ as Saviour but their lives give no evidence of Christianity.

"We desperately need Christian men in our village who will build Christian homes and furnish Christian leadership. Pray that men and boys who have made professions of faith will grow strong in the Lord."

From distant Africa, a missionary wife made this plaintive plea:

"Each month my husband tries to visit 11 churches with pastors and 13 preaching points without preachers. He travels more than 1,500 miles over rough, dusty roads. When the churches fail to grow, he feels he has failed somewhere.

"Pray God will give him enough wisdom, love, and patience to lead and inspire the African pastors and leaders. And pray, too, that he will have strength and good health."

From California a Baptist leader urged increased gifts by Southern Baptists so pastors in 10 communities won't need to spend their time in secular jobs to feed their families.

From Brazil a missionary family told Southern Baptists:

"As Christmas time approaches, we think more and more of you at home. Soon you will be giving your Lottie Moon Christmas offering. You cannot realize how the missionaries depend upon it to buy property, build churches and do many other things for which there isn't sufficient money through regular gifts.

"There is never enough money to meet all of the needs, but the more you give, the more you make possible. We are grateful to you for your generosity."

Testimonies such as these give Southern Baptists heart problems. Not coronary thrombosis but hearts that overflow with concern about the needs of people in this world.

Recognizing they can't go personally to every city and nation in the world to provide spiritual and physical relief, they resort to prayer and giving.

While times have changed drastically the last 2,000 years, the use of prayer and giving to express concern about the progress of God's plan for people hasn't.

Jesus was concerned about the needs of people when he prayed "Father, forgive them for they know not what they do."

Paul showed interest in the needs of people when he wrote the Christians at Corinth, "Every man according as he purposeth in his heart, so let him give; not grudgingly, or of necessity. For God loveth a cheerful heart."

Southern Baptists express that same concern today through a growing missions program to people throughout the world, supported by prayer and giving of Christians at home.

Just what does the expression, "Supporting World Missions Through Prayer and Giving," mean to Southern Baptists?

Prayer comes from a word in the Hebrew which signifies appeal, interpellation, intercession whereby men refer their own cause, and that of others, unto God as judge, calling upon him, appealing to him for right.

Thus prayer is communicating with God in behalf of the Southern Baptist program of world missions. Giving is supporting financially the Southern Baptist program of world missions.

World missions refers to the representative work that various mission programs in the associations, state conventions and Southern Baptist Convention conduct for churches. Best known in the Southern Baptist Convention are the Home Mission Board and Foreign Mission Board.

To support means to promote an interest or cause, or to keep something going.

B. PRAYER

1. Nature

Intercessory prayer—the act of pleading or making a request in behalf of another or others—was practiced in early biblical history.

Abraham interceded with God in behalf of the righteous in Sodom and Gomorrah.

James penned these famous words, "The effective fervent prayer of a righteous man availeth much."

In his second letter to Timothy, the Apostle Paul said, "I exhort that, first of all, supplications, prayers, intercessions, and giving of thanks, be made for all men."

The classic example of intercession was in the prayer of Jesus in John 17 as he looked down the course of time and brought the needs of all people to the attention of God.

Prayer and its attributes have been described many ways. Wrote William Law in *A Serious Call to a Devout and Holy Life:*

"There is no principle of the heart that is more acceptable to God than an universal fervent love to all mankind, wishing and praying for their happiness; because there is no principle of the heart that makes us more like God. . . ."

"Prayer is a very great thing," said Samuel H. Miller in *The Life of the Church.* "It is larger than a set of words, whether they be known by rote or uttered at the moment. It is more than kneeling, or the fingering of a rosary, or the pressure of our intention. . . . It is always the daring adventure of the spirit engaged in dialogue with God.

"Prayer is of great dimensions, and of great power, demanding all there is of man's existence."

Hugo Culpepper, director of the mission division of the Home Mission Board, describes prayer as yielding one's life and will to the Holy Spirit so as to become attuned to the will of God, seeing life and its values from Jesus' viewpoint.

"Only as the Holy Spirit is permitted to provide vision and dynamic in the lives of Christian people, will there be attained the depth of commitment and the degree of involvement requisite to the realization of God's redemptive purpose in the world."

2. Role of Prayer in Missions

Prayer played a prominent role in the lives of early Christians who prayed for the coming of the Holy Spirit and for Peter when he was in jail.

Paul prayed for the salvation of Israel, the maturity, insight and fidelity of all Christians, and that God would open doors so the gospel could be shared.

Through prayer the churches of Britain were prepared to accept the challenge of William Carey which led to the modern missions movement.

American churches caught the concept of world missions from a seemingly insignificant prayer meeting under a haystack at Williams College.

The importance of prayer as a means to enlist the power of God in a mission endeavor has captured the attention of Southern Baptists. This expression of faith from a missionary is an example:

"Since I asked you to pray for the beginning of Royal Ambassador work in our association in Nigeria, I want you to know your prayers have been answered."

Scores of missionaries testify to their increased awareness of God in their work on their birthday when Southern Baptists plead specifically for their causes.

3. Opportunities

Baptist men and boys receive varied opportunities to pray with the entire Christian fellowship, to pray in groups as part of the Brotherhood program, to pray as a member of a family and to pray individually.

a. *Prayer for Home Missions*

Annually in March Southern Baptists as a fellowship unite in prayer in behalf of mission work being conducted throughout the United States, Panama, Cuba, and Puerto Rico under the auspices of the Home Mission Board.

Known as the Week of Prayer for Home Missions, the event provides varied opportunities for Christians to pray for missionaries individually and mission progress as a whole.

The project encourages prayer for missions during worship services, at midweek prayer services, during organizational meetings of Brotherhood and Woman's Missionary Union, by families at home daily, and by individuals.

This extended prayer period quickens the sensitivity of Southern Baptists to needs in home missions which can be met often through gifts.

b. *Prayer for Foreign Missions*

The prayer emphasis each December for Southern Baptists is on foreign missions. At this time the welfare of missionaries in almost 70 countries and the general progress of foreign mission work become paramount in the prayers of Christians.

Begun as a prayer project by Woman's Missionary Union, the Week of Prayer for Foreign Missions now gets the attention of the entire Christian fellowship in many churches.

Often missionaries make pulpit appearances to open the week, followed by midweek prayer services and other church-wide prayer opportunities.

Persons also have opportunity to pray for foreign missions during organizational meetings, at prayer retreats, and at prayer breakfasts and luncheons.

Families and individuals also observe this special prayer period at home.

c. *Prayer for State Missions*

Southern Baptists are becoming increasingly aware of the need to pray for state missions. While the objects of prayer vary from state to state, the future of missions in each state serves as a common thread of concern.

d. *Prayer for Associational Missions*

With the larger role associations are assuming, particularly in highly populated sections of the nation, Southern Baptists are citing the needs of associational missions more frequently in prayer. The objects may include special ministries, starting of new churches, and the progress of the camping program.

4. CHALLENGE

Despite all of these opportunities, the true depth of prayer is often unreached. This untapped prayer potential can serve as a challenge for Christians.

Samuel Miller in *The Great Realities* expressed that hope this way:

"In the deep and consuming fire where the saint continually refines himself and hammers out the true beauty and strength of life, prayer becomes vividly real. Here the glow and light of man's spirit burns at its most intense pitch. This is the saint, where we see the dialogue of God and man most clearly, against whom we have revolted.

"Little wonder then that we don't know what to make of prayer. After all, this is not a disembodied harangue to be played off on a mechanical phonograph. It is possible only in a fully living man in conversation with the living God. We will not know what prayer means until we are able to take this frightening, disintegrating world of the twentieth century and bind it together in the quietness of the soul and without any publicity or pretentiousness embrace its tensions and contradictions in one harmonious living spirit. This would be to recognize a new kind of saint in our time.

"It is such a man who has real relationship with all the different aspects of human existence, from the deepest depths to the highest heights; who has not turned his back on science, or disdained art, or held philosophy in contempt, or looked at this tremendously blurred and confusing world in which we live and denied its reality; such a man who has stood in the middle of such a world with all its terrifying forces and terrible possibilities and has realistically and by tremendous imaginative grasp bound all of it together—this man is the man of prayer! It is in this man that one gets some semblance of what one might mean by prayer."

C. GIVING

1. Nature

"For ye know the grace of our Lord Jesus Christ, that, though he was rich yet for your sake he became poor, that ye through his poverty might become rich," wrote the Apostle Paul to the Christians at Corinth.

Citing the constraining love of Christ, Paul reminded that the Lord Jesus had gone from riches to poverty so people might go from poverty to riches.

Jesus has been called the greatest giver who ever walked this earth. On giving, Jesus said in Matthew 5:42: "Give to him that asketh thee, and from him that would borrow of thee, turn not thou away."

Dr. John A. Broadus said Christians need to give if merely to maintain their self respect because "our profession of faith in Christ demands it."

The foundation for the doctrine of stewardship which encompasses giving rests in the Old Testament.

Abraham and Jacob were highly involved in the giving process, as was Moses and the tribe of Levi.

It remained for the teaching of Paul in the context of the simplicity of New Testament practice to affirm clearly that the cause of Christian missions calls for support through gifts.

2. Role of Giving in Missions

Giving for the support of missions has many significant implications.

For instance, this act can be an expression of worship, recognizing the majesty and greatness of God and expressing devotion to him and his concern for the future of this world.

In another sense, giving for the support of missions permits a person to project himself directly into world missions. In a real sense, money is stored-up personality, expressing itself through missionaries, churches, and persons ministering to individuals in hunger, sickness, ignorance or other misfortune.

However, if the gift of a Christian in the compassion of love represents true self-denial and costly sacrifice, it becomes the spiritual force of redemptive love which the Holy Spirit can use in working through people in missions.

Giving for the support of missions should reflect obedience, faith and sacrifical devotion. As one writer expressed it, "Giving should be an expression of faith, the kind of faith that dares to be generous, that dares to commit oneself to worthy support of the worship and work of Christ."

Giving for the support of missions relates to the total stewardship of life. The giving of money is but one aspect of giving oneself. To the degree Christians recognize they belong to Christ, that they are stewards of the whole of life, and strive to be faithful in this stewardship, they will give worthily of material means to support world missions.

The spiritual potential of giving for the support of missions is vast. Besides building interest and concern for lost people and encouraging faith in and love for Jesus Christ, it motivates the Christian to accept more meaningfully the concept of Christian discipleship and sense of mission.

Southern Baptists have embarked upon an ambitious program of world missions which demands a new stewardship by Christians.

The implementation of this program has seen the number of missionary personnel increase into the thousands and the areas of work expand throughout the United States and into countries around the world.

If the plan is to succeed, the sacrifice of those who give their lives in mission service needs to be matched by sacrificial giving of the Christians at home.

3. Opportunities

In recent years Southern Baptists have sought to support world missions through giving through the Cooperative Program and special mission offerings.

a. *The Cooperative Program*

Off to an inauspicious start in 1925, the Cooperative Program has become the main channel of giving to missions for Southern Baptists.

Often called the lifeline of missions, this efficient denominational plan of financial support has put missionaries into the field almost as soon as they prepared themselves.

A genius of the Cooperative Program is that it enables every member of more than 34,000 Southern Baptist churches to contribute individually to what his state Baptist convention and Southern Baptist Convention are doing to advance the cause of Christ.

Here is how each Southern Baptist mission board, college, agency, and institution went about fund solicitation each year before the Cooperative Program was developed.

Agents were hired to ask for money from individuals and to receive special gifts from churches.

Offerings often became dependent on the weather and the number of persons and churches an agent could contact.

Often the response was determined by the approach, personality and voice of the agent rather than the merit of the cause.

The amount received seldom reflected the genuine needs of the institution requesting the money or the ability of Southern Baptists to give.

This method proved expensive since the agent's expenses had to come from the offering. Since income was seasonal, agencies often borrowed money to get through the lean months.

Advent of the Cooperative Program gradually eliminated the individual annual appeals, made possible giving on the basis of need, and insured regular, continuing support of Southern Baptist work.

Flexibility is another hallmark of the Cooperative Program. As needs of agencies and institutions change, the amounts allocated to them can be changed accordingly.

The money goes from the local church to the state Baptist convention which keeps a portion for state needs and sends the remainder to the Executive Committee of the Southern Baptist Convention.

This committee suggests the amounts each agency should receive and messengers to the annual session of the

Southern Baptist Convention alter and/or approve these suggestions.

b. *Special Offerings*

Special offerings for foreign, home, and state missions offer a way for Southern Baptists to give sacrificially.

(1) Lottie Moon Christmas Offering for Foreign Missions

Probably the best known special offering to Southern Baptists is the Lottie Moon Christmas Offering for Foreign Missions initiated on a small scale in 1888 by local societies of Woman's Missionary Union who wanted to send a missionary to China to relieve Miss Lottie Moon who hadn't received a furlough in 11 years.

The first offering attracted $2,833 in contrast to the more recent offerings totaling about 15 million dollars.

In 1918 the offering was named the Lottie Moon Christmas Offering for Foreign Missions. It is conducted by churches annually in December.

Initially the sole concern of women, the offering has become a church-wide event, offering men and boys an opportunity to play a vital role in their church's stewardship program.

(2) Annie Armstrong Easter Offering for Home Missions

An indebtedness of $25,000 at the Home Mission Board caught the attention of Woman's Missionary Union back in 1894 and led to the Annie Armstrong Easter Offering for Home Missions.

Opening with a "week of self-denial" to acquaint persons with the needs of home missionaries and the Home Mission Board, the women concluded the period with an offering.

The special offering was a success and became an annual event. In 1934 it took the name of Annie Armstrong Offering for Home Missions in behalf of the first secretary of Woman's Missionary Union. The word "Easter" was added in 1968.

Conducted annually in March, the offering provides about five million dollars toward financing home mission work.

(3) State Mission Offering

State mission offerings are conducted annually at various times throughout the year, many in September.

Use of the offerings varies from state to state depending on need. As an example one state used the offering to enlarge its Christian witness at state penal institutions while another offered a training, teaching and preaching ministry to the deaf. A third state uses the offering to supplement the salaries of mission pastors.

D. SUMMARY

The secret to effectively supporting world missions through prayer and giving is love for all people—all people.

The words of Samuel Miller expresses this concept eloquently:

"To understand another human life, even the simplest human being, will require a great deal of attention, insight, and imagination. If psychiatry has taught us nothing else, it has taught us that no man's consciousness can be marked off or set down in a five-minute conversation. It takes a long, persistent series of intense and willing interviews under the most hospitable observation if the exploration is to be meaningful. So love can validate itself, not in the blind thrust of an emotion, but only in the passionately intelligent understanding of the complex mystery of a human being.

"Our ideals can easily be mere disguises for our lack of

love. We love mankind in general but can't get along with our neighbors, or perhaps our own family.

"We will go to any cost to send missionaries to the ends of the world but we don't know how to communicate graciously or gently with the tradespeople at our very door. This substitution of a general idea is nothing but a sham.

"To substitute such vast, empty, comfortable abstractions for the embarrassments of real relationships with people leads to hypocrisy, however popular it may be in certain sanctified places.

"If we cannot love our neighbor, it is high time we admitted it, and started from such honest statement of fact to do something with ourselves or with him, rather than covering up the whole thing by a painted subterfuge."

5. Helping the Church and Denomination

CHAPTER OUTLINE

A. PROVIDE ORGANIZATION AND LEADERSHIP FOR SPECIAL PROJECTS OF THE CHURCH

1. The Meaning of Special Projects
2. Relationships in Conducting Special Projects

B. INTERPRETING THE WORK OF SOUTHERN BAPTISTS

1. Why Interpret?
2. The Work of the Church
3. The Work of the Denomination

• Each program organization has distinctive tasks. For Brotherhood, they are to teach missions, engage in mission action, and support world missions through prayer and giving.

At the same time each program organization serves as a resource for two other tasks. They are (1) provide organization and leadership for special projects of the church, and (2) provide and interpret information regarding the work of the church and denomination. Sometimes these tasks are referred to as special projects and channeling.

The two tasks enable the church to use its organizations to plan for a particular activity and to inform the membership of its work. This approach eliminates the need for special committees. At the same time a church using its program organizations can quickly inform a higher percentage of its members.

A. PROVIDE ORGANIZATION AND LEADERSHIP FOR SPECIAL PROJECTS OF THE CHURCH

It is important to recognize the difference between church projects and the ongoing work of a church. If a church is to fulfill its mission on earth there are basic ongoing activities that never cease. These ongoing activities are a part of the nature of a church. Three such activities find expression through the Brotherhood program, (1) teaching missions to all men, young men, and boys, and (2) engaging in mission action, and (3) supporting world missions through prayer and giving.

From time to time a church may wish to accelerate these ongoing activities by promoting additional related activities which last only a short period of time. Such short-term activity is identified as a project.

1. The Meaning of Special Projects

A special project is a short-term activity which has a fixed beginning and ending time and supports one or more church programs.

Special projects are a part of a total work of a church, not ends in themselves. They should be planned and performed always with church approval.

a. *Short-term*

Special projects come at a stated time in a church's work. Though they may be repeated from year to year, they are not continuous. It is the attempt of a church to accelerate or focus attention on an important phase of the church's work for a short period of time. An example is a church revival. Usually a church plans a revival with the purpose of reaching the unsaved people in the community. Reaching the unsaved is an ongoing activity of the church. During a revival efforts to reach the unsaved are intensified for a short period of time.

b. *Related to the Ongoing Program*

As a church performs its basic, ongoing program of work, it becomes desirable at times to lift out requests of ongoing work and amplify them. When a segment of work is singled out for special emphasis, that emphasis is called a project. An example is the commitment of men to service for short periods of time in areas of the United States where Baptist work is weak.

c. *Supports Ongoing Program*

A special project gives new meaning or a new thrust to the ongoing program of work in a church. An example is in the area of evangelism, specifically a revival. For such projects the Brotherhood organization is placed at the disposal of the church for specific work it wants done.

2. Relationships in Conducting Special Projects

Each church program organization is available to help the church with special projects. For many projects, all organizations will work together.

Leadership for projects should be assigned to the organizations whose primary tasks relate to the project.

Teamwork provides a church with a tremendous force for its work. A spirit of unity and interest for the overall task of the church is created when the programs of a church are fused.

B. INTERPRETING THE WORK OF SOUTHERN BAPTISTS

1. Why Interpret?

One of the main duties of a church is to keep its members informed about its work. The nature of church polity requires a well informed and committed membership. When churches are part of a democracy governed by the congregation it is necessary to keep every member informed on all of the work of the church and the denomination. Otherwise, uninformed members would not know how to govern themselves. However, the proper understanding of a church's work creates a strong bond of interest and participation.

The task of providing and interpreting information about the work of a church and the denomination rest on the five organizations—Brotherhood, Sunday School, Training Union, Woman's Missionary Union, and Music Ministry.

The vehicles these programs use are curriculum plans, activities, miscellaneous articles, and verbal reports.

In a sense, church organizations are channels, serving as a conduit through which information flows. This process can eliminate the need for additional organizations in a church.

2. The Work of the Church

In channeling, Brotherhood serves the church in various ways. One way is by sharing information. Through the meetings of Baptist Men and Royal Ambassadors, Brotherhood is able to keep its members well informed on the work of the church.

Normally this information is of a mission nature which permits men to perform more meaningful service.

Another valuable medium in channeling is what may be called promotional channeling. This is a step beyond providing information through an announcement. Some areas of church work require periods of promotion such as the church stewardship emphasis or January Bible Study.

When such events are planned by the church council, the Brotherhood director shares in the planning and also assumes responsibility for carrying out his commitments. The director will make plans with the leaders and officers of Baptist Men and Royal Ambassadors to insure the success of the church proposals. Many times these efforts will require promotion through bulletins, letters, posters, interest centers, and commitment cards. In this type of channeling a church has the full support of the Brotherhood program.

The Brotherhood director has the job of also communicating to the total church information about that portion of work Brotherhood does. These opportunities occur in meetings of the church council and the congregation.

3. The Work of the Denomination

Brotherhood has an important role in interpreting the work of the denomination.

The denomination is represented by three major groups: the association, state convention, and the Southern Baptist Convention. They exist to help the churches. These denominational groupings assist in two ways—by providing materials and resources which will help a church carry on its work and by doing for the church what it cannot do alone.

In the Southern Baptist Convention there are 17 agencies which exist to serve the churches. Each of the 17 agencies needs to interpret its work to the churches of the Southern Baptist Convention. The agency desires either to tell about the help it has to give to a church or what it is doing in behalf of a church. Only a few have corresponding organizations in churches. Thus they must depend upon existing church organizations to serve as channels. The Brotherhood is one of those channels.

In channeling, the agencies use the five program organizations—Brotherhood, WMU, Sunday School, Training Union, and Music Ministry. Each of the five program organizations has a supporting organization in the association, state convention, and Southern Baptist Convention.

The Brotherhood Commission works closely with the Convention agencies, using sections of its magazines for channeling purposes. *Brotherhood Builder, Baptist Men's Journal, Guide, Probe, Probe* (*Leadership Edition*), *Crusader* and *Crusader Counselor* periodically have feature stories, reports, and general articles on the work of the agencies of the Southern Baptist Convention.

Most of the study material provided in Brotherhood publications for the churches is planned in consultation with the Foreign Mission Board and Home Mission Board. In this way the two mission boards are able to communicate their work to the churches.

Field engagements of the denominational personnel offer additional means for channeling other programs. Personnel of Southern Baptist Convention agencies are given opportunities to speak at assemblies, workshops, and institutes when their participation is appropriate to the emphases of these field engagements.

6. The Brotherhood Organization

CHAPTER OUTLINE

A. WHAT IS THE BROTHERHOOD ORGANIZATION?

1. Principles of Organizing
2. The Brotherhood Organization
3. Suggested Organizational Patterns

B. HOW TO BEGIN A BROTHERHOOD PROGRAM

1. The Church Takes Action
2. Elect a Brotherhood Director
3. Train the Brotherhood Director
4. Begin Brotherhood Work
5. Begin Age-Level Units

C. THE BROTHERHOOD DIRECTOR

1. Qualifications
2. Duties
3. Election

D. THE BROTHERHOOD COUNCIL

1. Membership
2. Duties
3. Meetings

• The element of organization in Brotherhood is designed to provide an orderly arrangement of responsibilities assigned leaders and members for carrying out Brotherhood tasks. Organization is based on two elements—program structure and relationships.

A. WHAT IS THE BROTHERHOOD ORGANIZATION?

1. Principles of Organizing

Some organizing principles which may help churches in determining the Brotherhood organization they need are:

a. *The Principle of Purpose*

The organization should have a clearly understood purpose with every essential function represented. It is difficult to divide the work, group related activities, define and delegate responsibility and authority, and coordinate the work until one knows what must be done.

b. *The Principle of Efficiency*

Only the organization needed to perform the essential actions of the identified tasks should be established. Permanent organization becomes necessary only when there is sufficient continuous work to justify its existence.

Terminal organization (committee or individual assignments) should be established to conduct those temporary projects or jobs which cannot be done efficiently by permanent organization.

Organizational patterns should reflect simplicity, adaptability, and flexibility.

c. *The Principle of Specialization*

The organization should be established on the basis of specialization. Each element of the organization should receive work according to its specialization. By focusing on a similar group of activities, specialized knowledge and skill can be used better.

d. *The Principle of Authority and Responsibility*

Responsibilities of all components and members of the organization should be clearly defined. Authority to act should be delegated commensurate with the assigned responsibility. To assign authority or responsibility without the other is to create an untenable position.

e. *The Principle of Decision Making*

The organization should allow those who are affected by decisions to have a part in making them. Decisions must be made at a level high enough to represent all those affected, but as near as possible to the unit that will have to abide by the decision.

f. *The Principle of Coordination*

For maximum coordination the organization should provide for a free flow of communication. Coordination is concerned with synchronizing and unifying the actions within the organization. The lack of a clear understanding of exactly who does what leads to poor coordination. The ideal time to bring about proper coordination is in the planning stage.

2. The Brotherhood Organization

The Brotherhood organization is a church's vehicle for carrying out its mission program for men and boys. It may be as simple as one man seeking to involve men and boys in study and action and support without formal meetings and activities. It may be to provide several age level units for Baptist Men and Royal Ambassadors. In either case, the process should be designed to meet the mission needs of the church's men and boys.

There are two basic parts of the Brotherhood organization; (1) general administration, and (2) age-level organizations.

The general administration of a Brotherhood organization is the responsibility of the Brotherhood director and the Brotherhood council. The duties of the Brotherhood director and the description of the Brotherhood council are on pages 98-101.

The age level organizations are designed according to the recommended grading-grouping plan of the Southern Baptist Convention.

Children's Division (boys in grades 1-6)	Royal Ambassadors (in Crusader chapters)
Youth Division (boys in grades 7-12)	Royal Ambassadors (in Pioneer chapters)
Adult Division (high school graduation and up)	Baptist Men

Chapter 7 has a more detailed explanation of these age level organizations.

3. Suggested Organizational Patterns

The following patterns suggest the way a Brotherhood program can be organized. Some churches will only need a Brotherhood director. Others will need only one age level unit such as a Crusader chapter or a Baptist Men's unit. Still others will need a unit in all three divisions, while some churches will need several units in each division.

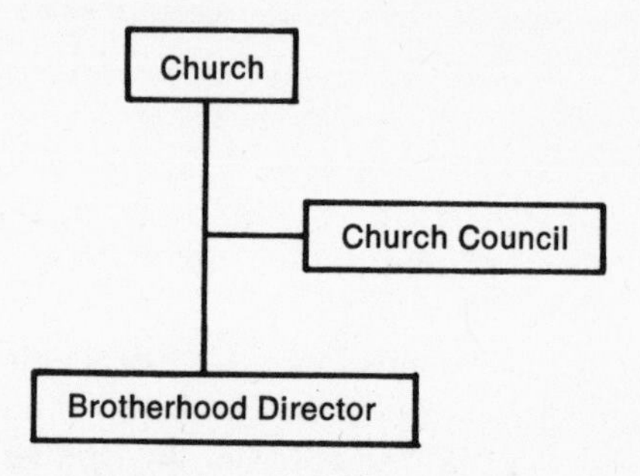

Pattern One consists only of a Brotherhood director who has the sole responsibility of helping the church provide a mission program for men and boys. He should make every attempt to organize age level units. Although age level units are not the only way to involve men and boys, experience has shown that it is a very good way.

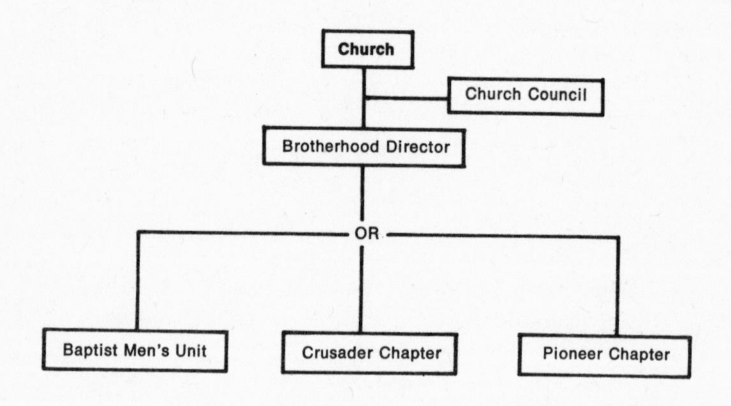

Pattern Two is the suggested approach for churches needing only one age level unit. It may be a Baptist Men's unit, a Crusader chapter or a Pioneer chapter. At least five men or at least 10 boys and a capable leader are considered necessary for an age level unit. In this pattern the Brotherhood director may serve as president of Baptist Men or as Royal Ambassador counselor until other leaders are enlisted and trained.

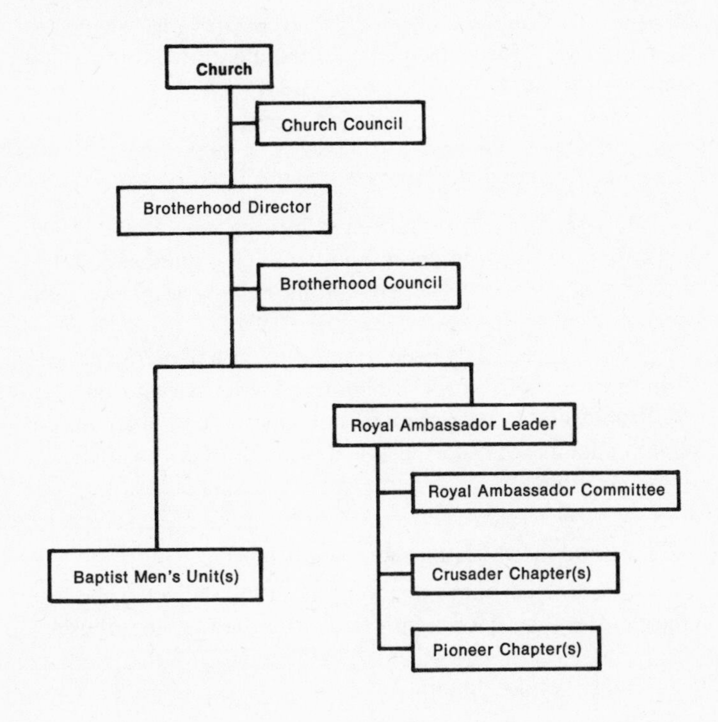

Pattern Three is suggested when there is at least one unit in each age division. This pattern calls for a Royal Ambassador Leader to administer Royal Ambassador work. It also calls for the formation of a Brotherhood council to coordinate Brotherhood work.

B. HOW TO BEGIN A BROTHERHOOD PROGRAM

Churches may already have a mission program for men or boys without a formal Brotherhood organization. It may consist of an occasional sermon on missions, an annual study of a mission book, or involvement in a mission offering or mission preaching station. A Brotherhood begins when persons attempt to formalize these efforts in a more effective and meaningful way.

These suggestions may be followed:

1. The Church Takes Action

A church becomes interested in beginning Brotherhood work by learning of the need and value of missionary education and mission involvement for its men, young men, and boys.

After interest has been aroused, efforts should be made to inform the entire church about the objective and tasks of the Brotherhood program. Before further action is taken, the church should vote to establish this phase of its total educational program.

2. Elect a Brotherhood Director

The Brotherhood director should be elected by the church. He should be nominated according to the church's policy for electing the other general church officers, such as the Sunday School director.

3. Train the Brotherhood Director

Basic training of the Brotherhood director is an essential step in beginning Brotherhood work. This person holds responsibility for initiating, coordinating, and evaluating the Brotherhood program. Basic planning guidance is in *Brotherhood Builder,* a quarterly magazine for this officer.

Before beginning work, the Brotherhood director should study this book carefully. He should also be familiar with *Baptist Men in Missions,* the methods book for Baptist Men, and *Royal Ambassadors in Missions,* the methods book for Royal Ambassador Leaders.

4. Begin Brotherhood Work

A Brotherhood director may begin a program to involve men and boys in a mission program even before age level units are organized. In some churches, especially small or new ones, a Brotherhood director may lead in mission projects while attempting to organize age level units.

The Brotherhood director should work with the WMU director in efforts to involve men and boys in church-wide mission study projects. He will also want to plan activities just for men and boys.

5. Begin Age Level Units

The Brotherhood director should lead in establishing age level work. That means determining the need for particular units, selecting leaders according to the church plan, and training them.

Suggestions for beginning Royal Ambassador work are found in *Royal Ambassadors in Missions.*

Suggestions for beginning Baptist Men's work are found in *Baptist Men in Missions.*

C. THE BROTHERHOOD DIRECTOR

1. Qualifications

To fulfill the requirements of his office, the director needs to have outstanding qualities. He should be:

a. *A Consecrated Christian*

The director must be a man of deep religious faith and beyond question as to his conversion, dedication to Christ, and reputation in the community. He also should be a man of prayer.

b. *A Loyal Member of His Church*

The church is the creation of Christ through which his work is performed. The director must be committed to the church, striving to see that Brotherhood is fitly joined to the work of the body of Christ, his church (Ephesians 4:16). It was said of Jesus that he "loved the church, and gave himself for it" (Ephesians 5:25). Such a devotion to the church must characterize the director.

c. *Deeply Concerned About Missions*

Unfortunately, too many people have a concept of missions that only relates to the people "in far away places with strange sounding names." Thankfully, this concept of mission work is diminishing. People with a genuine interest in mission work readily see that missions is the realization of God's redemptive purpose in Christ through human messengers to all people. The man who is to lead men and boys in missionary education and mission involvement must have compassion for all people.

d. *A Leader of Men and Boys*

The two words for any leader of men and boys are love and understanding. Men are quick to sense superficial attitudes and insincere interest. They will not follow a leader who pretends concern for them, but reflects domination.

The director must show an interest to work with men in a team effort. He must carry his responsibility as one who serves rather than one who wants to be served.

An understanding of boys is also necessary. He must understand boys as they are with a desire to help them become great men of God.

e. *Able and Willing to Work with Others*

The work of a church is not fragmented into little parts that exist for themselves. All of the organizations, committees, leaders, and members exist for the total work of a church. This means the director must plan and work with leaders of other church programs. The result is cooperation.

There is outward and inward cooperation. The Brotherhood director will cooperate in all that the church wants to accomplish. There also will be inward cooperation with the leaders of Baptist Men and Royal Ambassadors. The success of the director depends on how well he works with others.

f. *Able to Administer His Work*

The director will spend most of his time administering Brotherhood work. Hopefully, he will use qualities of good leadership in guiding the work of men and boys toward Brotherhood goals. For example, the director will not say "Get going!" but rather "Let's go!" He will not give orders, "Here's what I want you to do," but will ask, "How can we work together to achieve objectives?"

2. DUTIES

The duties of the Brotherhood director are extensive. The more basic ones follow:

- Directs the Brotherhood program (including both men and boys) of the church. The Brotherhood director should have a general understanding of the total Brotherhood program and the work of the two organizations, Royal Ambassadors and Baptist Men. A study of *Royal Ambassadors in Missions* and *Baptist Men in Missions* will provide this understanding.
- Interprets the church tasks to be carried out through the program. The Brotherhood has three

basic tasks. They are (1) teach missions, (2) engage in mission action and, (3) support world missions through prayer and giving. The task of interpreting information regarding the church and denomination is shared by all programs.

- Represents the program on the church council. The church council function is to plan, coordinate, and evaluate the total program of a church. The Brotherhood work should be a part of this process.
- Interprets church council assignments to the Brotherhood council. Periodically the church will ask Brotherhood units to conduct special projects. The Brotherhood director will need to assign these projects and make sure they are completed.
- Reports status of the program periodically to the church. The Brotherhood director should make monthly reports to the church on the activities of units. Reports should include number of men and boys enrolled and participating.
- Leads in organizing needed units for both men and boys. The Brotherhood director should seek to establish the necessary units to involve as many men and boys as possible.
- Coordinates the work of multiple units of Baptist Men.
- Recommends and enlists workers required by the proposed organization. Additional workers are always needed in Baptist Men and Royal Ambassador work. Growth is usually dependent upon the number of capable leaders.
- Guides Brotherhood workers to an understanding of their responsibilities. The training of Brotherhood leaders is an important responsibility. Study of the basic books and related material will prepare men to lead. The associational Brotherhood program will provide assistance.

- Coordinates the ordering of Brotherhood literature and supplies according to church plan. The Brotherhood director should see that each unit has the necessary materials for its work while not overlooking his own needs.
- Serves as chairman of the Brotherhood council. As chairman of the Brotherhood council the Brotherhood director should see that the functions of the Brotherhood are completed.
- Appoints a member of council to serve as secretary for council meetings.
- Works with WMU director in coordinating the mission program. Because the WMU and Brotherhood have the same mission tasks there is need to coordinate their work. This may be done in the church council or in separate meetings as necessary.

3. Election

The best way to select a Brotherhood director is to use a church-elected nominating committee. The church may instruct its nominating committee (elected annually in most churches) to bring the nominations for all church officers, including those for Brotherhood director, to the congregation for approval.

The nominating committee will want to seek the leadership of the Holy Spirit in finding and enlisting leaders.

The first approach to a prospective leader is very important. The nominating committee representative should contact the prospective director individually, outlining Brotherhood work and the duties of the director. A prayer with the prospective director and the promise to continue to pray with him until his decision is made are appropriate. Usually the prospective director should not be pressed for a decision until he has given much thought to the matter.

After the nominating committee has agreed upon a person to recommend, the following enlistment procedure is suggested:

a. Appoint person(s) under whom prospect will work to interview prospect.
b. Make appointment with prospect.
c. Pray for spiritual guidance in presentation.
d. Call on prospect.
e. Explain need.
f. Answer questions.
g. Assure church support, particularly in the areas of manpower, finances and cooperation.
h. Await decision.

If the enlistment of this person fails, the committee needs to select another prospect and repeat the steps.

If the church does not have a nominating committee, the men of the church may select the Brotherhood director, and present him to the church for approval.

D. THE BROTHERHOOD COUNCIL

1. Membership

Members of the council are church staff members, the Brotherhood director, and unit leaders.

a. *Church Staff Members*

As a member of the Brotherhood council, the pastor has an opportunity to help plan the general program of missionary education and mission involvement and evaluate it.

The minister of education is responsible for helping develop the educational program of the church and should be an active member of the council.

Other church staff workers may be substituted or included on the council.

b. *Brotherhood Director*

The Brotherhood director, who is responsible to the church for Brotherhood work, is chairman of the Brotherhood council and should lead the group in performing their duties.

c. *Unit Leaders*

The Brotherhood is composed of two basic units—Baptist Men and Royal Ambassadors. The leaders of these units—the president of Baptist Men and the Royal Ambassador Leader—are also members of the council.

If a church has only one unit, the work is normally planned by the unit leader, the Brotherhood director, and pastor.

d. *Invited Members*

From time to time the council will find it necessary to invite other church leaders to share in the planning. These leaders may include the director of audio-visual education, the church librarian, chairman of an emphasis committee, minister of music, or the chairman of the missions committee.

2. Duties

a. *Planning*

(1) Plan Actions to Help Reach Church Goals

These actions will relate to the goals and strategies of the church and will supplement the actions planned and developed in each unit.

(2) Review and Coordinate Program Plans

Actions planned in the units will be coordinated by the council to eliminate overlapping and improve the overall work.

(3) Develop Program Emphases

Whenever possible, Brotherhood work will relate to the emphases of the church. For example, if the church plans to stress stewardship during a certain quarter of the year, the council will develop plans for the units in keeping with this emphasis.

(4) Review Plans for Use of Resources

Detailed planning may include resources. These resources may involve transportation for the Royal Ambassadors to special events, the need for young men in a youth revival, or the need for homes for community prayer services.

(5) Make Definite Work Assignments

Each suggested action requires assignment to an appropriate unit.

b. *Coordinating*

The work of the units must be coordinated if the Brotherhood program is to go forward. Coordination means to pull together all of the plans of the units into a harmonious whole. The council should:

(1) Coordinate Actions Involving More Than One Unit

For example, Baptist Men may plan a project to witness and minister to the blind. This project may require participation by Royal Ambassadors. Such action would be coordinated through the council.

(2) Coordinate Special Projects

For example, when Royal Ambassadors plan man-and-boy night, the council should assign actions for each unit.

(3) Coordinate Organizational Planning Involving New Units, Space, and Equipment

A good example is a church which has a Baptist Men's unit but wants to organize Royal Ambassadors. The Brotherhood council would ask a committee of Baptist men to carry out initial steps for starting Royal Ambassadors or ask the church to appoint a Royal Ambassador committee.

c. *Evaluating*

Periodically, the council needs to review the work of the Brotherhood to make sure it remains true to the objective, goals, and tasks of the church.

When plans fail to produce expected results, the council will want to evaluate the plans and adjust them.

Churches vary in size and resources so organizational structures must be flexible. That means the council will need to study constantly the organizational procedures and suggested changes.

3. MEETINGS

a. *Frequency*

The rule is to meet as often as necessary to plan, coordinate, and evaluate the work of Brotherhood. One session each quarter seems logical in most cases.

b. *Duration*

The length of a meeting is determined by the amount of work to be accomplished. Two hours should suffice.

c. *Location*

Planners may meet in the church building, a home, or at a retreat site, depending upon the desires of the individuals.

7. The Units of Brotherhood

CHAPTER OUTLINE

A. ADVANTAGES OF THE DIVISIONS

1. Provides for Proper Grouping of Members
2. Provides for Normal Changes
3. Provides for Church Assignments
4. Provides for Flexibility
5. Provides for Proper Relationships

B. BAPTIST MEN

1. Relationship to the Church's Mission Program
2. Grouping Baptist Men into Units
3. Administration
4. Enlisting, Recording, and Reporting
5. Resources

C. ROYAL AMBASSADORS

1. Need for Royal Ambassadors
2. Organization of Royal Ambassadors
3. Administration
4. Methods
5. Resources

• When I became a man I put away childish things."

These words by the apostle Paul are a commentary on the ever-changing individual.

In recognition of the differences in maturity, interests, attitudes, and mental, physical, social and spiritual characteristics of persons, the Brotherhood program is divided into three divisions. These three units are designed to bring together men and boys into congenial groups and at the same time appeal to the spiritual interests of each.

The three divisions are Baptist Men (18 and older), Pioneer Royal Ambassadors (grades 7-12), and Crusader Royal Ambassadors (grades 1-6). There are several advantages in dividing the work this way.

A. ADVANTAGES OF THESE DIVISIONS

1. Provides for Proper Grouping of Members

The Brotherhood program relates to all of the men and boys (school age and older) of a church. To bring about the most effective work this audience is divided into age groups with similar interests and goals.

2. Provides for Normal Changes

The three divisions of Brotherhood were developed with the understanding they would provide for normal changes in people.

Physical, mental, and social changes occur throughout life. Boys pass through several pronounced changes in becoming men. Fortunately, all normal individuals of the same age experience approximately the same effect of maturation and social influences, which takes care of changes within the age groupings.

3. Provides for Church Assignments

The three Brotherhood divisions exist to serve the church. Through such groupings the church can assign work to be performed.

4. Provides for Flexibility

Churches may begin Brotherhood work by starting with any one or more of the three divisions. Once the church has organized a unit, it should continue with plans to provide all of the divisions of work. The flexibility of the units allows a church to begin and maintain Brotherhood work based on need.

5. Provides for Proper Relationships

The units are inter-related appropriately, with the Brotherhood council serving as coordinator of Brotherhood. However, at the same time, each unit can make an individual contribution to the work of the church.

B. BAPTIST MEN

Baptist Men is the name used to identify adults in the Brotherhood program. Baptist men is made up of men who are high school graduates or are 18 years of age and older and are members of the church. The unit is designed to involve men in the mission program of the church.

1. Relationship to the Church's Mission Program

The men of the church become concerned about missions and involved in missions as they become more informed about the subject. One of the main purposes of the Baptist Men's unit is to teach missions to men.

As men become informed about missions, their next step is to get involved in missions. The mission action program provides this opportunity for involvement. In this program men seek to extend the work of the church beyond its membership to persons of special need and circumstance.

Besides study and involvement through mission action, the men of the church express their commitment to support missions through prayer and giving.

Finally, Baptist Men participate in the mission program of the church by communicating information about the work of the church and denomination.

2. Grouping Baptist Men into Units

To achieve their purpose, Baptist Men organize themselves in groups called Baptist Men's units. Several criteria are used to determine these unit groupings.

The number of Baptist Men's units needed depends upon the number of men within the church. Where enough men are available to have multiple units, each man will be encouraged to take part in the unit nearest his interest or needs.

The interests of men vary according to age. In keeping with this principle, the Brotherhood Commission provides guidance for the following groups: Baptist Young Men (18-29), Median Baptist Men (30 to retirement), and Senior Baptist Men (retirement and older).

Another way men may be grouped is on the basis of available time. The suggested procedure is to determine the time when the men of the church are able to participate in missions and organize units to meet at those times.

New units of Baptist Men are organized when the need arises and resources are available. The Brotherhood director normally takes the responsibility.

The basic steps in starting a Baptist Men's unit are to create and secure interest in the work, organize for the work, train the officers to understand the work, plan the work, enlist men to do the work, and involve men in the work.

3. ADMINISTRATION

The officers of a Baptist Men's unit include the president, vice-president, secretary, Mission Study Leader, and Mission Activity Leader.

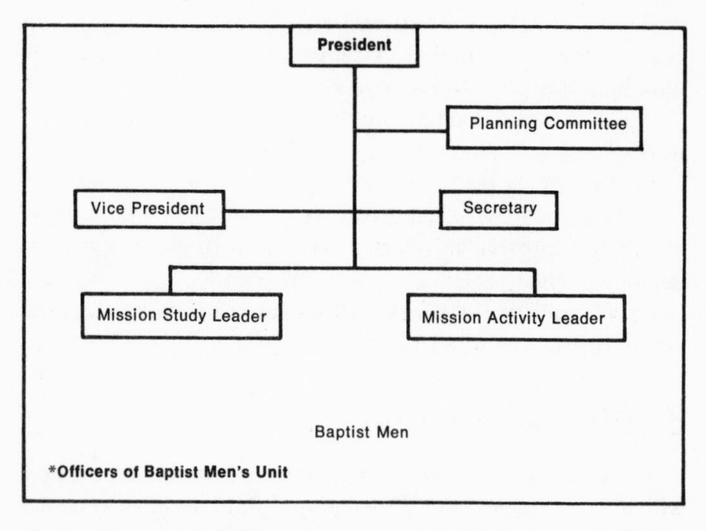

They are members of a planning committee which is responsible for initiating, conducting and evaluating the work of the unit. The planning committee receives suggestions and assignments from the church, via the Brotherhood council while seeking to provide programs and activities which will challenge the men to greater participation in missions.

The planning committee has the responsibility of seeing that the work supports the purpose of the Baptist Men's unit and contributes to the overall program of the church.

4. Enlisting, Recording, and Reporting

Every adult man member of a church should be encouraged to participate in the mission program of the church. Appropriate records and reporting process are available for determining whether or not the men are participating.

5. Resources

Baptist Men in Missions, by Clyde L. Davis, provides basic information, including methods for organizing and conducting the Baptist Men's program in a local church.

Curriculum materials for the unit meetings are provided in *Baptist Men's Journal* and *Guide,* published by the Brotherhood Commission.

Additional personal assistance and resource materials are made available through *Brotherhood Builder,* the associational Brotherhood program, the various state Brotherhood offices, and the Brotherhood Commission of the Southern Baptist Convention.

C. ROYAL AMBASSADORS

Royal Ambassadors is that part of Brotherhood through which a church provides a mission program for boys in grades 1–12. It is composed of the Crusader Royal Ambassadors for boys in the Children's Division (grades 1-6) and Pioneer Royal Ambassadors for boys in the Youth Division (grades 7-12).

Through Royal Ambassadors a church seeks to develop in boys a Christlike concern for all people, an intimate knowledge of how Christian fellowship is being extended at home and abroad, and a hearty participation in all efforts to enlarge this fellowship of Christian faith until it covers the earth.

This concept is the basis for the Royal Ambassador pledge which states:

"As a Royal Ambassador I will do my best:

To become a well-informed, responsible follower of Christ;

To have a Christlike concern for all people;

To learn how the message of Christ is carried around the world;

To work with others in sharing Christ; and

To keep myself clean and healthy in mind and body."

1. NEED FOR ROYAL AMBASSADORS

Royal Ambassadors makes three significant contributions to the work of a church.

a. *Reaches Boys Through Boy-Centered Activities*

This mission program capitalizes upon the characteristics and interests of boys in involving them in the world-wide ministry of a church.

b. *Strengthens the Work of a Church*

The educational program of a church is strengthened through a mission program for boys. By helping boys serve Christ through their churches, a Royal Ambassador chapter can become an introductory training program for future church leaders. Strong churches require dedicated, well-trained mission-minded men of every profession. The best time to mold the life of a man is while he is still a boy.

c. *Helps Minister and Witness to a Lost World*

A major responsibility of churches is to send out and support missionaries. Through Royal Ambassadors Southern Baptists seek to instill this responsibility in boys. Specifically, Royal Ambassadors teaches boys about missions and leads them to put missions into practice. It also builds mission interest in boys by enlisting their prayer support for missions and encouraging them to provide financial support for missions.

2. Organization of Royal Ambassadors

Because of the difference in the characteristics, needs, and interests of boys at different stages in life, Royal Ambassadors is divided into two divisions, each providing opportunities for experiences in missions.

a. *Crusaders*

The name Crusaders identifies the mission program for boys in grades 1-6. It suggests enthusiastic, eager, earnest, willing, and alert boys banded together to serve the cause of Christ.

Symbolic of this group is the Crusader shield which provides the background for Crusader pins. It stands for faith in Christ and signifies that the life and teachings of Christ guide Crusaders in their daily lives.

b. *Pioneers*

The name Pioneers identifies the mission program for boys in grades 7-12. This name suggests the adventuresome spirit which is characteristic of boys this age. Through this program boys receive new opportunities to serve Christ in missions.

Symbolic of this division is the Pioneer badge, a shield enclosed by a gold rim. The shield stands for faith in Christ and signifies that the life and teachings of Christ guide Pioneers in their daily lives. The rim represents God's unending help available to Pioneers.

2. Administration

The administration of the mission program for boys can be seen by carefully studying the chart below:

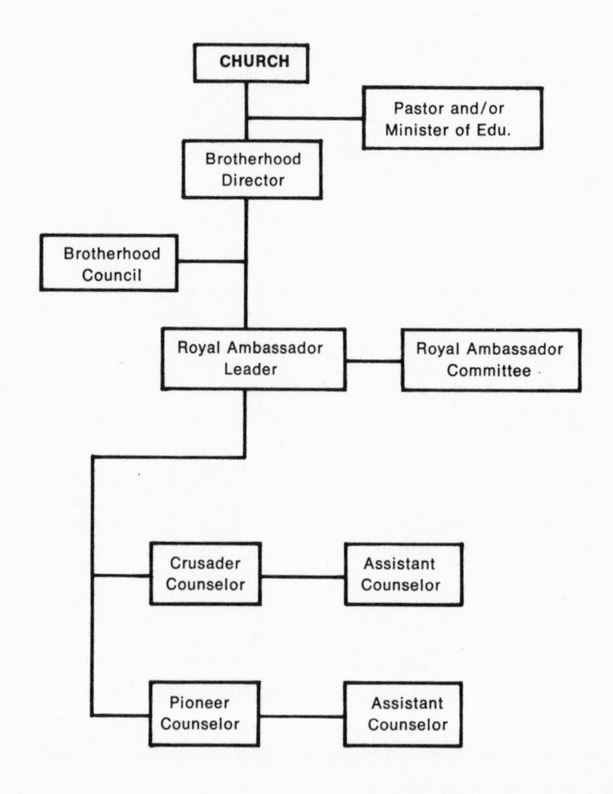

a. *The Royal Ambassador Leader*

The Royal Ambassador Leader is a church-elected officer who, with appropriate help from the Brotherhood director, leads in planning, directing, evaluating, promoting, and enlarging the church's mission program for boys.

As coordinator of all Royal Ambassador work in a church, the Leader serves on the Brotherhood council.

The qualifications of a successful Royal Ambassador Leader calls for an exceptional and dedicated Christian man. Heavy administrative responsibilities prevent most Royal Ambassador Leaders from serving well as counselors. In churches where there are more than three chapters in a division, the administrative duties may require the services of a Crusader Leader and a Pioneer Leader in place of a Royal Ambassador Leader.

b. *The Royal Ambassador Committee*

The Royal Ambassador committee is composed of counselors and resource persons. These resource persons assume specific responsibility in such areas as training, promotion, enlistment, advancement, recreation, and camping. They also have the responsibility of keeping the program church centered.

Each member of the committee should have a personal interest in the program. At the monthly committee meeting the interest of the committee should be stimulated as each chapter counselor submits his report.

c. *Chapter Counselors and Assistants*

Counselors work directly with the boys. They have the responsibility of involving boys in Royal Ambassador activities and leading them to make the Royal Ambassador pledge a part of their lives.

3. METHODS

Royal Ambassadors use the following methods to achieve the Royal Ambassador pledge:

a. *Participation in the Chapter Meetings*

Through effective leadership, chapter experiences provide opportunities for accepting and respecting the other fellow, for sharing responsibilities in planning and evaluating, for abiding by the decision of the majority, and for sacrificing for the cause of Christ.

These experiences are provided through chapter meetings planned around suggestions in the boys' periodicals.

b. *Participation in the Advancement Plan*

Advancement plans are based on the characteristics, needs, and interests of boys. They include methods of achieving activities, followed by recognition for this advancement. The counselor, parents, and boys determine the activities which will be most helpful to each boy and to the chapter. Specific guidance is in the boys' manuals.

c. *Participation in Mission Activities*

Royal Ambassadors seek to serve their church and community. Through mission activities they become conscious of Christian responsibilities. The boys learn about their church and how it serves the community and the world when they help others. Mission activities also help adults become more aware of the part boys can play in the mission work of the church.

d. *Involvement in Meaningful Relationships*

Through Royal Ambassadors boys establish important relationships with parents, adult leaders, their church, and with other boys.

4. RESOURCES

Basic information on the mission program for boys is found in the book, *Royal Ambassadors in Missions,* by Jay Chance. Detailed information about leading each division is in *Crusader Counselor's Guide,* by Frank Black and Frank Lawton, and *Pioneer Counselor's Guide,* by John Scales.

Crusader materials are provided in *Crusader,* monthly magazine for boys in Crusader chapters and in *Crusader Counselor,* quarterly publication for chapter counselors.

Pioneer materials are in *Probe,* monthly magazine for boys in Pioneer chapters, and *Probe* (*Leadership Edition*) for counselors and officers of Pioneer chapters.

Guidance materials for the Royal Ambassador Leader and committee members are in *Brotherhood Builder.*

Other important resource material is available free from the state Brotherhood department.

History of Brotherhood Work

• Southern Baptists have long realized the worth of men in the advance of the cause of Christ. Realizing this worth, the Southern Baptist Convention moved years ago to provide for men an avenue through which they could be challenged to make their contributions to the work of their churches and denomination.

1906—The idea for a Laymen's Missionary Movement germinated in the mind of John V. Sleman, Washington, D. C. businessman, while he was attending a Student Volunteer Convention in Nashville, Tennessee March 2. As he heard student volunteers speak about the purpose of their lives, this thought passed through his mind: "If the laymen of North America could only have the vision of obligation that fires these students, they would arise in their might and provide all the funds needed for this enterprise."

Mr. Sleman's idea came into full bloom November 13–14 in New York City at the centennial of the Haystack prayer meeting. At that time a group of laymen of various denominations discussed the need for enlisting men in the work of foreign missions.

They passed a series of resolutions and elected a committee to consult with the various foreign mission boards regarding a program to: (1) educate and interest men in missions; (2) devise a plan for world evangelization; (3) appoint a commission of laymen to tour the mission fields and report their findings to the churches. Thus began the Laymen's Missionary Movement in America. Within the year that followed, many denominations formed their own Laymen's Movement.

1907—Southern Baptist men met in Richmond, Virginia, May 16, prior to the Southern Baptist Convention, to consider steps Southern Baptists should take regarding the Laymen's Missionary Movement. They recommended to the Convention that a Laymen's Missionary Movement under the auspices of the Southern Baptist Convention be launched.

In a meeting later in the week the Southern Baptist Convention voted into existence the Laymen's Missionary Movement. This movement was the forerunner of Brotherhood work. Its major purpose was set forth in the recommendation of a special committee appointed by the Convention:

> ". . . Through this agency, to bring more directly to the attention of our laymen the purposes and spirit of this movement . . . and to stimulate the zeal and activity of our laymen to a more thorough consecration of their time, prayers, and means to the glory of God in worldwide evangelism . . . ." (1907 *SBC Annual,* p. 46)

The Convention elected an Executive Committee composed of nine men to guide the Laymen's Missionary Movement and named Baltimore, Maryland, as the city where offices of the movement were to be located. (1907 *SBC Annual*)

1908—In its first annual report to the Southern Baptist Convention, the Executive Committee of the Laymen's Missionary Movement stated that the method of work for the movement was to determine the needs of the field, to scatter this information and to stimulate the securing of adequate funds to finance the great missionary undertaking. To achieve this end the committee pointed to the need of "the creation and circulation of a suitable literature." (1908 *SBC Annual,* p. 26) J. T. Henderson, first executive secretary of the Laymen's Missionary Movement, assumed his responsibilities on July 1.

1910—The Convention adopted the report of the Executive Committee of the Laymen's Missionary Movement which included the statement: "We would again endorse the policy outlined one year ago, placing special emphasis on: (1) missionary education; (2) tithing as the minimum in our giving and at least as much to missions as to church expenses; (3) the every-member canvass; and (4) the weekly system of giving. There is little hope, however, outside of the general diffusion of missionary intelligence; laymen need to have enlarged vision and this comes only with knowledge. . . . The movement is seeking to create interest and give men information by missionary education, through tracts, journals, addresses, sermons, and mission study classes." (1910 *SBC Annual,* pp. 5–6)

1913—The work among the men was more clearly defined by the Executive Committee of the movement in its annual report:

> "The committee has sought to be aggressive during the past year in advocating the principles for which this movement stands; the promotion of missionary

intelligence among the men; a proper recognition of the obligation of Christian stewardship; a systematic effort to deepen the piety of business—a constant emphasis upon the priority of Christ's claim upon the thought, time, talent, and treasure of Christian men; and unswerving loyalty to the local church and its divinely appointed leader, the pastor. . . ." (1913 *SBC Annual,* p. 22)

1915—The Convention's Committee on Woman's Work recommended that "the men through the Laymen's Committee undertake as soon as practicable to organize and train our boys (Royal Ambassadors) over 12 years of age and to develop among them leaders and workers in missions for years to come."

(1915 *SBC Annual,* p. 31) Headquarters moved from Baltimore, Maryland to Chattanooga, Tennessee.

1916—The movement was continuing its emphasis on missionary education through the use of tracts, periodicals, books, lectures, and sermons, and mission study classes. (1916 *SBC Annual,* pp. 23–30). The movement led in an effort to help raise funds to pay off the indebtedness of $276,000.00 against the two mission boards. The men raised $23,123.64 (1916 *SBC Annual,* p. 8)

1919—The report of the Laymen's Missionary Movement said numerous churches were organizing men's unions and some expressed the preference for the name "Baptist Brotherhood" instead of "Baptist Men's Union."

1920—Laymen's Missionary Movement contributed much time and effort to the promotion of the 75 Million Campaign.

1921—Annual report revealed that churches were organizing Brotherhoods.

1922—Stewardship and missionary education continued to be the primary emphasis of the Laymen's Movement. (1922 *SBC Annual,* pp. 61–64)

1923—Laymen's Movement report included information that the organization was publishing literature for the Brotherhoods and promoting study classes for deacons. (1923 *SBC Annual,* pp. 47–50)

1924—The Convention approved the report that stressed "the idea that these organizations (Brotherhoods) should promote fellowship, intelligence, and spirituality in order that the laymen may be prepared to render more effective service in connection with all the enterprises of their church and denomination . . . Report recommended that the general secretary give special attention to perfecting a more thorough organization in each of the states . . . ." (1924 *SBC Annual,* p. 52)

1925—Men's conventions were conducted in nine states; in other states associational or regional rallies were held. All stressed the obligations of laymen "in connection with missions, stewardship, systematic giving, evangelism and Christian education." (1925 *SBC Annual,* p. 88)

1926—The Convention approved the recommendation from the Laymen's Executive Committee: "That more attention be given to personal evangelism by men . . . this would call for prayer groups among the men . . . devotional readings from their Bibles . . . a course of training that would fit them to render effective service as soul-winners." (1926 *SBC Annual,* pp. 101–104) The Convention voted to change the name of the organization from the Laymen's Missionary Movement to Baptist Brotherhood of the South. (1926 *SBC Annual,* pp. 101–104)

1934—A Brotherhood report revealed a continued emphasis on deacon training and development. (1934 *SBC Annual,* pp. 64–67)

1937—The annual report revealed a large increase in the number of Brotherhoods and in the demand for Brotherhood quarterlies and other literature. (1937 *SBC Annual,* pp. 23–27)

1938—Lawson H. Cooke, associate secretary, succeeded J. T. Henderson as general secretary. Headquarters of the Baptist Brotherhood of the South were moved from Knoxville to Memphis.

1939—The annual report of the Brotherhood stated its definite purpose was to mobilize, organize, vitalize, and utilize the manpower of the church. It adopted the slogan, "A Million Men for Christ." It listed 10 Brotherhood objectives which included, "A debtless denomination by 1945." (1939 *SBC Annual,* pp. 99–102)

1943—The annual Brotherhood report showed cooperation between State Brotherhood and Woman's Missionary Union Departments in promotion of Royal Ambassador work. (1943 *SBC Annual,* pp. 110–113)

1950—The Convention, acting upon recommendation of its Executive Committee, changed the name of the "Baptist Brotherhood of the South" to "Baptist Brotherhood" and gave the work among men Commission status. (1950 *SBC Annual,* p. 39) This action elevated the status of the organization from that of a standing committee to a Commission.

1952—George W. Schroeder, associate secretary, succeeded Lawson H. Cooke as executive secretary of the Brotherhood Commission.

1953—The annual report of Brotherhood Commission stated executive officers of this agency and state Brotherhood secretaries worked out a new organizational pattern for the enlistment of young men, ages 17–24, in Brotherhood work.

1954—Convention adopted the report of its special committee recommending that Royal Ambassadors, Southern Baptists' missionary education organization for boys, be transferred from Woman's Missionary Union to the Brotherhood Commission. Recommendations included:

> "That the Royal Ambassador program continue to be a missionary organization.
> "That the Convention allocate adequate funds to the Brotherhood Commission for the promotion of this work." (1954 *SBC Annual,* pp. 46-47)

1955—Brotherhood Commission assumed from Woman's Missionary Union the sponsorship of the Young Men's Mission Conference at the Convention-wide assemblies. The Commission sponsored two missionary tours of laymen, one into Cuba, the other into South America. (1955 *SBC Annual,* pp. 309–313)

1956—Convention, upon recommendation of its Executive Committee, approved the Charter of the Brotherhood Commission. The charter reveals that the Brotherhood Commission is to exist:

> ". . . For the purpose of promoting the work of said Convention among the men and boys who are members of the Southern Baptist churches affiliated with it. The major duties of the Commission will be to seek to discover the talents of the men and boys of the Southern Baptist churches, challenge these individuals to action, and utilize their talents for Christ. To achieve these ends the Commission will (1) develop and promote a program of work directed toward the enlistment of men and boys in the life work of their churches, (2) produce necessary publications, tracts, and other materials through which they will become acquainted with the work of their denomination, and (3) seek to promote and conduct such meetings as may be necessary to build concern among the men and boys in the matter of spreading the Christian message to the farthest reaches of the world. . . ."

1956—Reports from the states revealed that during 1955, 24,118 boys attended Royal Ambassador encampments. Of this number, 5,490 made decisions either in accepting Christ or dedicating their lives to him. (1956 *SBC Annual,* p. 312)

1957—The publishing of *Ambassador Life* was transferred to the Brotherhood Commission by the Woman's Missionary Union. National Conference of Southern Baptist Men held in Oklahoma City, Oklahoma, attracted 6,282 men. Two mission tours involving 87 men were made to Mexico.

1958—Brotherhood enrollment had grown to 347,187 men and number of churches with Brotherhoods had climbed to 11,657. Royal Ambassador organizations were in 9,922 churches with 162,724 boys enrolled. (1958 *SBC Annual,* p. 382)

1959—Brotherhood announced that plans were being made for reworking the organizational structure of the church Brotherhoods and for an enlarged Royal Ambassador program. (1959 *SBC Annual,* pp. 383–387) The Brotherhood Commission began publishing *Ambassador Leader,* a quarterly magazine for men who work with boys. . . . Commission seeking to provide avenues through its publications for other boards and agencies to impart information to Brotherhood and Royal Ambassador constituency . . . Convention-wide Royal Ambassador Congress held in Fort Worth, Texas in 1958 with 8,500 boys in attendance.

1960—New Brotherhood program introduced to churches. Areas in which men were encouraged to study and work included Royal Ambassadors, Christian witnessing, personal stewardship, and world missions. With the new program the Brotherhood Commission began publishing the *Brotherhood Handbook,* an annual publication providing a year's programs and activities for church Brotherhoods.

1961—New Royal Ambassador program introduced to the churches. It initiated new techniques aimed to attract and hold the interest of boys in a deeper study and practice of that which is involved in missionary education. Brotherhood defined world missions and missionary education to be:

> "World missions is the active effort of sharing Christ with all peoples in every part of the world with the purpose of leading them to personal faith in Christ in obedience to his will."
> "Missionary education is the sum of the efforts of a Baptist Brotherhood to develop in boys a Christ-like concern for all peoples; an intimate knowledge of how Christian fellowship is being extended at home and abroad; and a hearty participation in all efforts to enlarge this fellowship of Christian faith until it covers the earth."

Annual report of the Brotherhood Commission also told of enlisting 550 men to participate in pioneer area mission work in seven states.

1962—Annual report of the Brotherhood Commission stated the first regional Brotherhood enlargement campaign was held May 13-18 in Birmingham, Alabama. Purposes were to train Brotherhood leadership and build stronger and more effective Brotherhood organizations. 1,400 men were enlisted to participate in pioneer area mission work.

1963—Brotherhood Commission reported 30,000 boys attending established summer camps and 828 men serving in pioneer mission areas. It also reported initial recruitment of 1,000 men to take part in the West Coast Laymen's Crusade in 1964.

Brotherhood enrollment climbed to 385,897 men and 242,166 boys were enrolled in Royal Ambassador chapters. Commission reported continued efforts in enlisting men to participate in the 30,000 Movement. (1963 *Book of Reports,* p. 143)

1965—The Southern Baptist Convention adopted the following objective for the program statement of the Brotherhood Commission:

> "The objective of the Brotherhood Commission is to support the Southern Baptist Convention in its task of bringing men to God through Christ by fostering programs that will assist the churches in their tasks of leading men, young men, and boys to a deeper commitment to missions, to a more meaningful prayer life for missions, to a larger stewardship on behalf of missions, and to a personal involvement in missions."

1968—The Fourth National Royal Ambassador Congress attracted more than 10,300 boys and their counselors to a missions-packed three days August 13-15 in Oklahoma City.

1970—The Brotherhood program was expanded to include boys 6-8 in Royal Ambassadors with the advent of the new Southern Baptist grading-grouping plan. Administration of the plan at the point of materials development called for the Brotherhood Commission to prepare all of the missionary education guidance materials for boys in the Children's Division (boys in grades 1-6). Five new periodicals were introduced under the titles of *Crusader, Crusader Counselor, Probe, Probe* (*Leadership Edition*) and *Brotherhood Builder.*

Personal Learning Activities

QUESTIONS

Chapter I

1. List four characteristics which help describe the nature of a church.
2. What is the mission of a New Testament church?
3. List the five functions of a church.
4. Identify the four elements in the objective of Brotherhood.

Chapter II

1. List three values of teaching missions.
2. Identify the four major sections which make up the content for teaching missions.
3. List two main mission learning opportunities for men and boys.
4. Tell how a study of the Bible in Sunday School contributes to better mission understanding.

Chapter III

1. Identify the four basic needs of a person which Christians have an obligation to meet.
2. Define mission action.
3. Identify six major categories which provide target groups for mission action.
4. List the four elements of a mission action program.
5. List two ways of conducting mission action.

Chapter IV

1. Describe the role of prayer in missions.
2. Identify four opportunities for prayer for missions.
3. What is the Cooperative Program?
4. List three special offerings most churches give for missions.

Chapter V

1. Give three characteristics of a special project.
2. Identify a special project of the church which usually requires the efforts of all organizations.
3. What is the value of interpreting the work of Southern Baptists.
4. Identify the three major groups making up the denomination.

Chapter VI

1. Identify the two basic parts of the Brotherhood organization.
2. Name the five steps in beginning a Brotherhood program.
3. List three qualities of a model Brotherhood director.
4. Identify the members and three main duties of the Brotherhood council.

Chapter VII

1. List four advantages of dividing Brotherhood work into divisions.
2. Identify the officers of a Baptist Men's unit.
3. Who are Pioneers and Crusaders?
4. Identify the curriculum magazines used by members of Baptist Men, Pioneers, and Crusaders.
5. Identify the magazines prepared for leaders of Baptist Men and counselors of Crusaders and Pioneers.